Too Hard to Forget

ALEXEI NAVALNY, YULIA NAVALNAYA AND THEIR VISIONS

By Dr. Kofi Aninakwa

Dedication

This book is dedicated God and God's children who are well thoughtful persons fighting for a safer democracy for their countries and the world at large over several centuries now. The political legacy and impact of Alexei Navalny and Yulia Navalnaya energized a big portion of Russian society. His anti-corruption work has forced several changes to the administration and methods of Russian policy often garnering more negative responses from Russian authorities. These changes and the exposing of corrupt individuals and plots have only retreated him to unsuitable and dangerous jobs and forced libel suits, perhaps the most controversial cases were his "Russia for the Russians" campaign and movement of the now defunct and politically unsuccessful "People's Freedom Party".

Acknowledgements

The world will be a better place thanks to people who want to develop and lead others. What makes it even better are people who share the gift of their time to mentor future leaders. Thank you to everyone who strive to grow and help others grow.

Visions cannot be buried, they will continue to visualize and sprout across the globe. Alexie Navalny and Yulia Navalnaya, kudos.

Preface

Alexei Navalny was born and raised in Kiev, Ukraine. Nevertheless, he maintained strong family ties with Russia. His maternal grandfather, Y. V. Rudnitsky, was a Russian revolutionary and a member of the Red Army and a prominent dentist. Navalny's father, A. L. Navalny (born 1942), is from the Pskov region and graduated from a medical institute. He was a retired military officer who worked in a health clinic. His mother, L. I. Navalnaya, has a degree in history and is a professor at the Russian State University for the Humanities.

Navalny's brother, Oleg, is an associate professor of political science at the Moscow State Institute of International Relations. Navalny said in an interview for The Guardian, childhood. He was popular at school and had many friends. He and his friends formed a music band, but Navalny considers it a failure and regrets never having learned to play any instrument. His first love was Anastasia, with whom he fell in love at the age of 15.

They connected on social media years later. Navalny also mentioned another notable person in his childhood, Aleksandr Andriyevsky, his wrestling coach. He trained Navalny for about four years until Navalny got a knee injury. Throughout his childhood, Navalny attended a Russian-language school, where he excelled in class. He has also shared that he was shaped by his family's history. His great-grandfather, A. I. Ivanov, was a colonel in the Imperial Russian Army and was executed by the Bolsheviks.

Table of Contents

PART ONE

ALEXEI NAVALNY

1. CHILDHOOD

His father, Anatoly Navalny, was an officer in the Soviet army, and his mother, Lyudmila, was a housewife. His family was middle class, and he had a brother, Oleg, who is 3 years younger than he is. After several relocations, his family settled in Kubinka in 1997. This was where Alexei finished secondary school and passed his college entrance exams. In a personal blog post written in 2008, Alexei said that neither of his parents had any political inclinations, nor in response to a comment questioning how a KGB agent's son would not follow his father's example.

He confirmed that his parents had nothing to do with the KGB - the comment was based on a spelling mistake in a newspaper heading which mentioned Alexei's family. His grandparents were also ordinary citizens - his maternal grandfather was a tailor who worked in a garment factory and his paternal grandfather was a welder.

The family had no links with politics. Alexei and his younger brother were brought up in the local tradition of respect for the family, parents and teachers. His parents were very dedicated to their children's education, and the focus was on academic success from an early age, which Alexei achieved with 'excellent' grades. In fact, Alexei's mother gave up work in order to look after him after he failed an important exam, although Alexei describes this as 'nonsense', saying that she had been considering giving up work anyway. On the other hand, he did say that his mother had supported him - "she never got angry about my low grades and never put pressure on me."

1.1. Education

Navalny went to the local state school #381. This is where he met his future wife, Yulia. His academic record there was average, in his own words. He went on to study law in the Russian capital, Moscow. Whilst in his second year, Navalny was in charge of the Moscow branch of the liberal Yabloko party's youth wing, known as Yabloko Youth. At the same time, in 2001, he was elected to the federal council of the party. The next year, whilst still in his final year of the law degree, Navalny created and started an attorney position at the Moscow regional arbitration court's commercial law division, at the age of 26. This was, however, after he founded a political and civil rights movement called "The People" which fought for decent housing provision and other social issues. Just as Navalny was finding his academic feet in the law, his political activities began in earnest.

2. ACTIVISM

In 2008, Alexei Navalny started to participate in public activism. His early activism focused on the political youth movement and local environmental issues. However, Navalny's public influence and fame significantly increased after he initiated large-scale anti-corruption campaigns. In the 2010s, Navalny began to found and lead various non-governmental organizations with a focus on investigation and exposure of corrupt practices among the high-level Russian politicians and state-owned corporations.

For example, in December 2011, a few days after the parliamentary election in which the ruling party United Russia was accused of vote rigging, Navalny initiated a massive political campaign to organize tens of thousands of Russians in protests against the election results. He labeled the United Russia a "party of crooks and thieves" and launched a popular blog with the same name to mobilize Russian citizens and to collect donations for the anti-corruption activities. On July 18th, 2013, Navalny was found guilty in a criminal trial that claimed Navalny embezzled money during his service as an advisor to the governor of Kirov Oblast.

However, Navalny and many independent observers argued that the charges were politically motivated and the trial was held unfairly. The European Court of Human Rights eventually ruled that Navalny's and his co-defendant's rights to a fair trial were violated, and that both of them were "arrested and detained, and their liberty was restricted, for other reasons than conviction". In December 2016, the anti-corruption fund co-founded by Navalny released the largest investigation report up to that day, which accused the Russian Prime Minister Dmitry Medvedev of controlling personal assets through a complex network of non-profit funds and shell companies.

The report also revealed the luxurious properties and residence that belong to Medvedev and his close relatives. It gained widespread attention in Russian society and provoked wide criticisms against Medvedev. Navalny's lawyer confirmed that he would run in the 2018 presidential election if he could successfully register and become a candidate. On December 25th, 2017, the Central Election Commission of Russia officially barred Navalny from the 2018 election due to his prior conviction in the criminal case. His supporters claimed that the decision was politically motivated and intended to suppress political competition.

2.1. Anti-Corruption Campaigns

Now I shall explain the anti-corruption work carried out by him. Alexei Navalny and the Anti-Corruption Foundation have been conducting investigations involving corrupt practices in the highest echelons of power in Russia since 2011. The Foundation shares its research and findings with all interested organisations and citizens through the media and alternative reports on internet sites.

According to the results of official investigations resulting from the work of the Foundation team, which were conducted directly as the result of appeals made to the relevant authorities by Alexei Navalny, hundreds of lawsuits have been won by private citizens and companies as a result, and hundreds of people have had unfair judgments made against them overturned on appeal. A special system for the continuous monitoring of court decisions was also established.

The main idea behind the Anti-Corruption Foundation was to provide people with access to the law, using legal procedures in order to change the situation and allowing people to feel personally empowered, rather than simply trusting that unforeseen moral change in current Russian public life will allow authorities to deal with corruption.

2.2. Political Protests

The first significant street protest that Navalny led was in the wake of the 2011 legislative elections, which saw Putin's party, United Russia, lose a significant number of seats in the Duma. Opposition leaders and electoral observers claimed that the election was marred by vote rigging. United Russia's reduced majority was viewed by many as a response to public reports of corruption and a lack of transparency in electoral politics.

Large anti-corruption demonstrations were organized by Navalny, and he later coined the phrase "the party of crooks and thieves" to describe United Russia. This phrase gained substantial traction within the opposition movement and beyond. Navalny was one of the key speakers and leaders of the 2011-2012 protests against Putin's third term in office, as opposition groups attempted unsuccessfully to unseat the authoritarian leader. In subsequent protests, and as anti-government demonstrations took place in the wake of the 2018 presidential elections, Navalny has been systematically arrested and detained by the Russian authorities. His brother, Oleg, and supporters and offices of his Anti-Corruption Foundation have all been targeted by the authorities in various criminal cases. T

his sustained legal pressure from the government has fuelled debate in the midst of critical moments in Navalny's political career about the legitimacy of his campaign, and his own eligibility to stand for office, on the one hand, and the space permitted to civil society and opposition groups, on the other. This theme has provoked international interest and widespread condemnation abroad of Putin's administration's approach to demonstrations and freedom of expression.

2.3. Investigative Journalism

Between 2008 and 2013, Alexei Navalny established himself as a prolific blogger and investigative journalist. He investigated and published articles on alleged corruption schemes at Russian state-owned companies. His work attracted significant numbers of readers and gained him a reputation as an anti-corruption activist. One of his most notable investigations concerned the Russian national airline Aeroflot.

Using women's names as search terms to navigate the database of a shadowy company, Navalny's team uncovered what they considered to be the laundering of stolen money to the tune of billions of rubles. The investigation focused on a query submitted under the name "Nadezhda Prusakova". By navigating through a series of companies, her name had led them to a curiously named business. They then used a similarly circuitous route from a number of other female names to trace a large number of suspicious payments that had been made to this company. Navalny's report included official Aeroflot documentation and named key employees of the company.

The work was praised as the first example of a blogger-driven investigation breaking the near-total control of state TV over the narrative of Russian political life. The findings of the reports were covered by international publications and were quoted in anti-corruption responsibilities at the Council of Europe. However, the publicity also attracted the attention of the authorities. In November 2011, the Investigative Committee of Russia conducted a series of raids on the Moscow-based offices of a number of opposition-minded NGOs.

The offices of Navalny's Fund to Combat Corruption were also searched and computer equipment was seized. Throughout the investigation by the police, Navalny remained undaunted. He claimed that the search was triggered by his high-profile work as an anti-corruption campaigner and that the authorities aimed to disrupt his activities. He also uploaded to the internet a video showing the arrival of police at his office. In it, a detective is heard warning Navalny that his actions may lead to being arrested.

The investigator has since publicly apologized for the comment. None of the charges made during the searches resulted in a conviction and the equipment was returned. The European Court of Human Rights later ruled that the period of seizures had been procedurally in breach of the right to privacy. More information can be found about this and other illegal investigative activities by the Russian authorities in the 'legal difficulties' section.

3. LEGAL TROUBLES

Finally, the work investigates Navalny's legal troubles. According to Navalny, the ruling party uses legal charges to stifle his political activities. His usual practice of being notified about a formal case against him through the mail has earned the nickname of eCases in Navalny's team. The work offers illustrative examples of the eCases. These legal challenges hardly escape the international community's attention, especially considering the background of politically motivated trials in Russia. I believe they would agree with my decision to devote a whole section on the legal troubles of Alexei Navalny in the work.

Finally yet importantly, the work and outreach of Alexei Navalny have been significantly impacted by such continuing legal challenges. Sometimes I feel like my journey in the section also mirrors that of Navalny to a certain extent. We both have gone through bitter moments, faced the fear of infringements on human rights and been pushed to the corners by the governments. I have used the similar picture at the start of this section as the cover image for this work. This picture shows us the police chopper following the crowd in one of the protests she just mentioned above.

The continuous struggle for equal human rights underlies every single appeal that is manifested by all the protesters' lookings up to the chopper. It implies a future still with hope and determination for a positive change. Every time I search for this work in my computer and see the cover picture, I cannot help having the passion pouring out from every pixel on the screen. Every segment and digit of this picture faithfully records the light of justice that never dies out and that would eventually demolish all the darkness of oppression, regardless of any intervening periods of time - my surging emotions never fail to occupy and inspire my heart.

His outspoken criticism of the Kremlin has made him a target for the government. Alexei is often arrested and jailed. Recently found guilty of fraud and in 2014 he received a suspended sentence in another fraud case.

3.1. Arrests and Detentions

The police have arrested Navalny on numerous occasions, often for organizing or taking part in political demonstrations without permission from the authorities. Most of these incidents have ended in administrative detentions of up to 30 days, but some have led to criminal charges. Navalny was first given a custodial sentence in December 2014, when he and his brother Oleg were convicted of fraud and money laundering in what was widely seen as a politically motivated trial.

However, rather than being sent to prison, he was given a suspended sentence of three and a half years, while his brother was jailed. A suspended sentence usually means that a person is not imprisoned, provided they follow certain rules and do not commit further crimes. Navalny believes that he received a suspended sentence because the authorities, fearing widespread protests and international condemnation over his imprisonment. On 22 June 2019, the police while walking from his home to the Moscow Anti-Corruption Foundation arrested Navalny.

The authorities said that the reason for his arrest was five unanswered calls from a bailiff. However, the European Court of Human Rights later found that the arrest was politically motivated and was designed to curtail anti-government demonstrations. The court ordered the Russian government to pay Navalny financial compensation.

3.2. Criminal Convictions

Mr. Navalny has a criminal record due to the conviction in the Yves Rocher case. It appears that Russian law did not then provide that a conviction for a serious non-political offense would disqualify a person from standing for election to the Russian legislature. However, in December 2018, the Central Election Commission refused to register him as a candidate for the election to the State Duma on the grounds that Mr. Navalny was not eligible.

He was disqualified because of the conviction, and the ECtHR pointed out that the relevant provisions barring a person from standing for election due to conviction and sentence were justified, as not all criminal convictions meant a deprivation of electoral rights. As noted in the ECtHR judgment, by the end of the main case, the applicant had served over one year in detention on remand, a sentence of five years of residence arrest, and had been subjected to multiple restrictive probation measures. According to the ECtHR judgment, the living conditions and access to legal representation were inadequate.

In the Yves Rocher case, a Russian court determined in February 2018 that Mr. Navalny embezzled funds acquired from the French cosmetics enterprise, Yves Rocher. The ECtHR held that the main reason for the Yves Rocher case was a legitimate one and not politically motivated. However, they found that the applicant had not had the opportunity to examine the case file regarding the initiation of the preliminary investigation, and that the courts had not provided sufficient reasoned decisions on the deprivation of his liberty.

Navalny is frequently convicted in criminal cases. A high-profile case was the Kirovles case, where he was convicted of embezzling lumber from a state-owned enterprise. Navalny has argued that his prosecution and conviction were politically motivated, and the ECtHR ruled that his rights were violated in the Kirovles case.

12

3.3. Poisoning Incident

On 20th of August 2020, Navalny fell ill during a flight from Tomsk in Siberia to Moscow, leading the airplane to make an emergency landing in Omsk, where he fell into a coma. A few days later, he was transferred to the Charite hospital in Berlin, Germany. The doctors who treated Navalny in Omsk have repeatedly claimed that there was no trace of poison in his body when he was in their care and that they saved his life.

However, the team of medics who treated Navalny in Berlin have stated that poisoning was the most likely explanation for his condition, and later, a specialized military laboratory in Germany confirmed that a "cholinesterase inhibitor" from the Novichok group was found in his body. Novichok is a nerve agent that was developed in the Soviet Union, and it has been used in various high-profile assassinations or assassination attempts in recent years, such as the poisoning of the former Russian double agent Sergei Skripal in the United Kingdom. Navalny emerged from the coma on 7th of September.

His team quickly organised for him to be medically evacuated to Germany for further treatment, and he was flown to Berlin by a non-commercial ambulance aircraft on 22nd of August 2020. On 15th of September, senior western political figures, such as the Chancellor of Germany Angela Merkel, publicly stated that Navalny was poisoned with a Novichok agent. The Russian government has consistently denied that it was involved in poisoning Navalny and has not opened a criminal investigation into the incident. However, the use of a military-grade nerve agent has been viewed by many as a sign that the attempt on Navalny's life was state-sponsored. The nature of the poison and the identity of those who ordered it must still be definitively established.

4. POLITICAL CAREER

Navalny's entry into politics dates back to 2011. It was in December 2011 that he founded the "People's Alliance". This was a non-systemic opposition party in Russia that was committed to promoting civil rights, social justice, and the rule of law. However, the Russian Ministry of Justice refused to register it as a political party. Navalny and the "People's Alliance" sought to contest the results in the European Court of Human Rights. However, the court found no violation of their rights. Furthermore, in July 2013, the Investigative Committee of Russia initiated a criminal case against Navalny on charges of defrauding a company of 16 million rubles.

He was found guilty in December 2014 and received a suspended sentence of three and a half years. Navalny's junior brother Oleg, who is also his business partner, was jailed for three and a half years. Navalny's supporters claim that the case was politically motivated. They argue that he was the only person to have been convicted for the alleged fraud. It is understood that the European Court of Human Rights has since ruled in February 2018 that Navalny was a victim of violations of his rights under the European Convention on Human Rights, namely his conviction was based on an unforeseeable application of criminal law and was arbitrary and manifestly unreasonable.

However, the Russian government disputes the court's judgment. This decision plays a significant role in restoring his political rights and clearing his criminal record. On 28 April 2017, the District Commission on Licensing of Moscow rejected Navalny's application to stand for the presidency. The commission said that he could not run for office because of his conviction. However, Navalny's name has been widely discussed inside and outside Russia as a potential candidate.

He is active in comparing his case with the case of the Russian president, Vladimir Putin. On 24 December 2017, a consultative council of the "People's Alliance" voted in support of boycotting the Russian presidential elections the following year. In the run-up to the 2018 presidential elections, Navalny organized a grassroots campaign. He declared that he aimed to fight for a place on the ballot paper; however, this ambition was terminated by the Central Electoral Commission of Russia.

4.1. Opposition Movement

In 2011, Navalny and other opposition leaders organized protests in response to election fraud and political corruption. These were the largest anti-government demonstrations in Russia since the fall of the Soviet Union. The movement brought issues of corruption and political freedom to the forefront of the public's attention. Despite the violent arrests and opposition, the group led by Navalny worked hard to advance an anti-corruption agenda in Russia. He started his own anti-corruption organization called the Foundation for Fighting Corruption.

The organization is known for its investigations of the highest-ranking Russian officials, revealing their ill-gotten gains and corrupt practices. The members of the group include some very authoritative people. For example, the chairman of the Foundation is Nikita Girikh, a former Russian opposition member of the Parliament and the Member of the political council of 'People's Freedom Party'. The head of investigation is Ivan Zhdanov, a Russian attorney and the Candidate of Legal Science. According to the official website, the Foundation uses "the best principles and standards of investigations to pursue corruption at different levels in Russian Federation".

The Foundation uses the technique of the crowd in the fight against corruption, which is a new and modern method to reveal the corruption. In addition to gathering information and evidences, Navalny and the organization also engage in legal proceedings such as suing the Prosecutor General's office for refusing to investigate First Deputy Prime Minister of the Russian Federation. As a result of the lawsuit, the court ordered the prosecutor's office to open the investigation. This and many other cases show that Navalny and the Foundation use different strategies, including the lawsuits and media, to engage in the fight against corruption.

These strategies have also brought them different levels of successes both in the court and among the Russian public. However, Navalny has paid a price personally for his political activities. He has been banned more than once to run for public offices. He has been arrested on many different occasions because of participating in demonstrations and rallies. In 2017, he was physically attacked by a group of people who poured a green antiseptic liquid on his face. The right eye of Mr. Navalny has sustained "chemical damage" as explained by his press secretary. Despite all these harassments and legal troubles, Navalny continues his fight against the corruption and repression in Russia.

He is generally recognized as the leader of the Russian political opposition. His influence is very significant, although his critics often dismiss him as a trouble-making opposition and his impact on the Russian politics is subject to future developments. Anyways does current president of Russia Vladimir Putin consider him and his political activity a threat? Alexander Baunov, a Russian foreign and defence policy expert, made an interesting analysis. According to Baunov, Tzar Peter I gave the permission for a limited criticism in the society but not to those who promote the general slogans 'Down with the Tzar!' and 'Enough of the Boyars!'. Navalny risks and often crosses this very thin line between an acceptable criticism and an unacceptable subversion in the eye of the government.

With this thin line in mind, and given the size of the country and the centralization of the authority, the impact of an opposition leader in Russia "depends on how much fear dominates public politics and public life." Also, given the legal environment that is resistant to change, "to be a leader in the modern, non-formal, and radical opposition equals to the willingness to be in and out of the jail" according to Baunov.

4.2. Presidential Campaign

In 2016, Navalny announced his intention to run for president in the 2018 election. Although Putin had not announced that he would run for re-election, most observers believed that he would and that Navalny would be running against him. Navalny began outlining his political platform early in 2017, calling for increased spending on healthcare and education and decreased spending on the military and law enforcement.

However, as he began to open campaign offices in the spring of 2017, he was arrested and accused of violating laws governing public demonstrations and of using unauthorized symbols of his presidential campaign. When he was convicted of these charges in a court in Kirov in early July of 2017, Navalny and his legal team decided to mount a challenge to the conviction in the European Court of Human Rights. But the day before the deadline to submit his paperwork to the Central Election Commission of the Russian Federation to be eligible as a presidential candidate,

Navalny unexpectedly announced that he was withdrawing his presidential candidacy, citing as his reason the refusal of the Russian government to allow him to run as what the international community would consider to be an authentic opposition candidate. Later in 2017, after a civil rights group spent months compiling testimony, documents, and video evidence from the Kirov trial, the group approached the European Court of Human Rights and filed a case on Navalny's behalf.

The European Court of Human Rights decided to prioritize the case and requested that the Russian government respond to the allegations, giving a deadline of April 2018 for that response. By the fall of 2017, it became clear that Navalny had not changed the outcome of his criminal case in Russian courts, as the country's Supreme Court denied his appeal and upheld the earlier decision. All possible domestic legal remedies had been exhausted, which meant that Navalny could take his case against the Russian government to the European Court of Human Rights. Overall, a battleground for the defense of democracy and human rights had been opened up between Russia and the international community through the courts.

4.3. Political Party

Navalny's most recent political activities include his role in the founding of the Russia of the Future Party. This is a liberal party that seeks to introduce progressive change to the Russian political system, advocating for objectives such as the implementation of political reforms, the reduction of government control over the lives of individuals, and the introduction of measures to combat official corruption. Navalny and his associates in the Anti-Corruption Foundation filed official papers establishing the party on 15th December 2012.

However, these papers were initially rejected by the Ministry of Justice. Navalny criticized the Ministry's decision as a reflection of the extent to which the machinery of state is used to stifle opposition and maintain the status quo. But having spent time traveling around Russia meeting other party members and seeking to promote and develop the Russia of the Future Party, plans were announced to hold a political rally in Moscow in mid-2013, as a way of both protesting at the lack of genuine political debate and diversity of views in Russia and also raising public awareness of the Party's aims and objectives. Professor Newell argues that the formal restrictions that the current political system places on the development of political parties, such as the requirement that they have a minimum number of members from different regions of Russia or the right to appear on various electoral 'tickets', works against opposition groups.

However, it is clear that the Government is very sensitive to opposition groups and parties and that the restrictions foreshadow a broader public discourse over corruption and the way the rule of law is operationalized in Russia. Over the summer of 2013, Navalny sought to develop the effective infrastructure that would be necessary for the Russia of the Future Party to function. He traveled to numerous cities in Russia to develop party structures and to attend rallies, whilst at the same party leaders attended different training sessions to develop their own skills in campaign strategy and in the use of social media for publicizing the Party's aims and objectives.

The goal was to prepare it for participation in political life in Russia by reaching out to people who saw the need for change but who didn't feel that there were any genuine channels through which their voices could be heard. By the end of the summer, the Party reported the successful completion of its membership campaign, in which it had sought to attract support from a broad cross-section of Russian society, and the first congress of the Russia of the Future Party was held in late August 2013. This brought together members from all over Russia and the Party passed its Charter and other foundational documents, electing its first Central Political Council and party officials.

Navalny was elected as Chairman of the Party and gave a speech in which he underlined that the Party is ready to take up the challenge of a new form of democratic politics, in which public opinion drives policymaking, provided that it had sufficient support from the Russian people. It was also used as a platform for the presentation of the Party's symbolic image - a white star surrounded by a blue ring. This is intended to signify the victory of honesty over corruption, with the idea being that the star's brightness will illuminate the path towards an honest and fair society. At present, the Party is small and has not yet experienced any electoral success. Prof Newell suggests that, without any MPs in the Duma and with Navalny remaining subject to legal hurdles in his efforts to stand for the Presidency, the homage the greater public support may prove difficult.

Nonetheless, he goes on to say that the initial obstacles to the Party's development are seen as secondary to a broader theme, namely that the Russia of the Future Party represents the aspirations and hopes of a new generation of Russians who want to live in a society in which the rule of law and participation in public life are.

5. INTERNATIONAL RECOGNITION

The day after he had been arrested in Moscow, Alexey Navalny saw with surprise his name on the charts of social networking: was also the most discussed topic on Twitter. It was enough to protest against the government of President Vladimir Putin and his video denouncing - one of the most famous opponents of his regime - to unleash an international chain of solidarity. In several cities in Europe and the United States, more and more personalities requested the release of the Russian activist. Decisions.

The popular blogger and anti-corruption lawyer has become the symbol of the protest movement against the Kremlin, which saw the largest mobilization in the country since the end of the 90s, when it was decreed the dissolution of the USSR. The Russian faithfuls follow it by launching an appeal on its website to support his candidacy, after collecting about 60,000 signatures, which will have to validate the electoral commission. His figure - is expected to deal with the current prime minister, Dmitri Medvedev - and his decisions in the coming months will have a major impact on the political scene.

At the international level, Mr Navalny has become known due to the series of popular videos in which he revealed several cases of high corruption in the country, targeting political leaders and influential businessmen. In 2011 he was sentenced to 15 days in prison for obstructing the investigation into the embezzlement of wood from the prestigious KirovLes. In the last year, he has suffered two convictions in two successive trials. First, in December, was sentenced to three and a half years suspended in the process KirovLes, despite a decision from the European Court of Human Rights in Strasbourg, which considered the sentence "manifestly unreasonable".

In February he accused St. Petersburg of fraud in another case that allegedly took place between 2008 and 2012 and, according to the accusation, caused a loss to the Russian state of about 10,000,000 euros. He denied those accusations and a hearing with prosecutors in his attempt to annul legal gut. The judicial decisions that have fallen on it are - he said 'subtly' - politically motivated and are "banal revenge." But still there is no final judgment and the campaign, he claims to be stuck since February in legal gut and condition of the movement of binding: it can no longer leave the Russian territory.

After a trial in February, was placed under review. And that's why he was arrested in early March. His brother, Oleg, was also convicted in the process KirovLes and sentenced to three and a half years in prison. The US State Department considered him a "political prisoner". The decision cripples the work of Team Navalny. "I think the Kremlin has made it absolutely clear in recent months, and perhaps the past year, that they did not see for us no longer as a dangerous tumor, but as an existential threat, which must be excised with all the force and no matter the law" says Mr Navalny.

He adds: "It is important to understand that the only legal base for being in power by Mr Putin in Russia - or for any autocratic power in the other world - is the support of the population, the love for you. And it must be shown that actually rocks the boat and demand change. And the Achilles heel of any empire - and Russia is no exception - is that you can not govern without the silent consent of the community.

And this silent consent has been refused. And the regime has nothing left but the application of force." His case has also attracted the attention of international organizations: Amnesty International has started a petition asking for his release, which has already collected over 50,000 signatures worldwide.

5.1. Awards and Honors

Navalny has been recognized for his political and social activism on multiple occasions. In 2011, 2012, and 2013, The Moscow Times named him as Russia's second most influential politician. He was the only non-parliamentary figure in the top 10 of the list until 2018. In 2012, he was awarded the title "Man of the Year" by GQ Russia. Amnesty International recognized Navalny as a prisoner of conscience in January 2014.

He was also named the European of the Year in 2016 by the European Parliament. In June 2019, Navalny received the "Courage in Journalism" award from the International Center for Journalists for his work on his YouTube channel providing political analysis and exposing corruption in Russia. On October 15, 2020, the World Leadership Alliance-Club de Madrid awarded him the "Democratic Courage" Prize. In an official statement, former US secretary of state Madeleine Albright praised Navalny as "an inspiration to people across the globe who are fighting against corruption and standing up for democracy" and hailed his "extraordinary courage in the face of extreme adversity". His "Democratic Courage" Prize was also endorsed and congratulated by the head of the World Leadership Alliance-Club de Madrid and former prime minister of Portugal António Guterres, who praised Navalny's leadership, his bold choices, and efforts in promoting his people's wellbeing and effective citizenship. On January 25, 2021, High Representative of the European Union for Foreign Affairs and Security Policy and Vice President of the European Commission Josep Borrell Fontelles, wrote on Twitter in support of Navalny, who was then arrested by Russian police. Navalny was awarded the 2021 Sakharov Prize for Freedom of Thought by the European Parliament on October 21, 2021. The prize was awarded to Navalny in "recognition of his fight for freedom, democracy and the rule of law in Russia, notably through his 'Anti-corruption foundation'". The European Parliament told of its hope that the award to Navalny would count as a guarantee for his release, and in dedication to all persons and organizations striving for freedom and human rights in the Russian Federation and the world at large. On November 11, 2021, the European Parliament adopted a resolution on the situation in Russia in which it demanded "the immediate and unconditional release of Russian opposition leader Alexei Navalny, as well as of all other persons arbitrarily arrested for demonstrating peacefully against the regime in Russia". On November 12, 2021, the Subcommittee on Human Rights of the European Parliament held together with the World Leadership Alliance - Club de Madrid a hearing dedicated to the situation of Navalny and human rights in Russia. Dr. Mohammad Tahir, senior fellow at Hudson Institute, urged the West to take a more assertive stance in confronting the Kremlin and supporting the Russian opposition and civil society. He suggested that the European Union could station peacekeepers in Crimea in order to raise the stakes for Russia and thus to exert diplomatic pressure in the field of human rights.

5.2. Support From World Leaders

Navalny's work has earned him recognition and respect around the world. Many notable public figures and political leaders have shown their support for Navalny's causes and bravery. For example, the United States, the United Kingdom, France, and Germany condemned the attack on Navalny's life and demanded a full investigation. The U.S. National Security Council has called for Navalny's immediate and unconditional release from detention. When Navalny was arrested at Sheremetyevo airport in Moscow in January 2021, the U.S. Department of State spokesperson declared that "the U.S. strongly condemns Russia's decision to arrest Alexei Navalny. We note with grave concern that his detention is the latest in a series of attempts to silence Navalny and other opposition figures and independent voices who are critical of Russian authorities." Similarly, after Navalny's trial and immediate imprisonment in a police station in February, there was a campaign for support of Navalny from members of the House of Representatives and Senate in the United States, initiated by Markwayne Mullin, who is the U.S. representative for Oklahoma's 2nd congressional district. In fact, not only the West, but also leaders and officials from countries in Asia and the Middle East like Japan, South Korea, Taiwan, Qatar, and Poland expressed their concern for Navalny's situation. For instance, when the Japanese daily Mainichi Shimbun reported about Navalny's poisoning and political activities, Kono Taro, who was the Minister for Foreign Affairs in Japan, voiced out his words about the necessity for Russia to provide clarifications. Despite Navalny's arrest and recovery, Putin still firmly denies the allegations of the Russian governmental involvement and criticized Western countries for their reactions towards the case. However, it is clear that as the world is paying attention to Navalny's persecution and the way the Russian administration adapted to the crisis, the international concerns and criticism put immense external pressure on Putin and his political regime.

6. IMPACT AND LEGACY

Navalny's role in leading the opposition in Russia and challenging the Putin government cannot be understated. As the most popular opposition leader, Navalny has been a thorn in Putin's side for years. Notoriously, in 2013, he was sentenced to five years imprisonment, seemingly in an attempt to neutralize his opposition movement. As a response, tens of thousands of people took to the streets and the protests were so significant that they actually led to a suspended sentence and release for Navalny. This is a clear example of the impact Navalny has had - his efforts have led to a significant political movement and an increased pressure on Vladimir Putin. Since his second time in prison, where he was again denied access to mainstream media, his popularity has surged online, particularly among young people. Even in prison, his team have been producing smart voting and anti-corruption videos and Russians have been taking the streets to protest his arrest in the last few days. It is clear that Navalny has changed Russian politics by creating a network of like-minded young people and setting the agenda with widespread protests. Social reform is a key part of Navalny's political beliefs and it is no wonder that his biggest legacy will probably be the effect he has had on the Russian public. He has changed the way Russians think about their power to bring around change and this will no doubt shape the countopro. This particular incident has sent Navalny to the hospital and on the 18th of March 2018, he was taken to a hospital in Moscow by ambulance suffering from an 'acute allergic reaction' which one of his doctors claimed could have been due to poisoning. This has attracted widespread international attention: German Chancellor Angela Merkel and US Secretary of State Mike Pompeo have publicly wished him a speedy recovery and have been calls for him to be allowed to travel to another country for treatment. This is not the first time Navalny has been a victim of poisoning. In 2017, he had to go to a Spanish hospital after an antiseptic dye attack that led to partial loss of vision in one eye. In terms of impact, it is clear that these shocking events have helped to publicize Navalny's work and his allegations against the Kremlin. It has only served to give him a platform from which to speak to a wider audience both in Russia and globally and may in fact have bolstered his supporters against the Russian authorities.

6.1. Influence on Russian Politics

When he was barred from the 2018 presidential election, due to a financial-crimes conviction that his advocates contended was politicized, he organized a boycott of the election and an army of volunteers who went on to campaign in most regions of Russia. By September 2020, his team had helped opposition politicians win a number of local elections, including several spots on the Moscow city council, after authorities allowed opposition candidates to run for the body, and the Siberian candidate from his party came within one percentage point of winning the governorship in the region. He advised his supporters on strategies for winning elections through his YouTube videos, such as by holding primaries to consolidate around a single opposition candidate, and his director of political activities, Leonid Volkov, told me that a training video Navalny's team produced on the subject has been translated into nine languages and is used by politicians in countries like South Africa and Myanmar. But Navalny has said on many occasions that "I think this whole election campaign is a special operation. And its main goal is to not let at least half of potential voters to go to the polls." His party was never allowed to register and most of its members, some of them, have been harassed and detained. He said he had a "pleasant shock" after the European Court of Human Rights last year ruled that Russia's repeated arrests of Navalny were politically motivated and breached his human rights. His team has recently begun focusing on a project to impose targeted Western sanctions—like travel bans and asset freezes—on members of Russia's elites close to Putin using the slogan "Navalny sanctions, not aesthetic sanctions" and a comprehensive website that lists more than

1,000 people to sanction. It reflects a kind of maneuver that he has been adapting in the past—instead of only doing something to appeal to his domestic followers; he's also trying to get some sort of reaction or get support from abroad, especially from the West.

6.2. Public Perception

Navalny's public perception has drastically changed throughout his political career. At first, during his legal troubles and before his significant political campaigns, he was mainly seen as a relatively obscure figure with rather niche interests in combating corruption. This slowly progressed to a more negative image, especially within the loyalist factions, after he started achieving a significant degree of notoriety in his activities and in 2011 began building connections with more established politically active organizations and leaders in light of his potential role as a long-term oppositional figure. This only worsened as he held more protest rallies and demonstrations, as mainstream state-controlled media organizations began producing more and more frequent and aggressive smear campaigns and negative coverage of both his actions and his character. Pro-Navalny protestors, especially in the 2019-2020 period, were often characterized by journalists in papers like Izvestia or Pravda as either being misinformed, manipulated, or even as violent criminals. This characterization ranged from ignoring instances of police brutality at the hands of violent public order units against neutral peaceful protestors, to the belittling and ridicule of the intentions and ideological goals of members of the movements that had begun to form around the call for political reform that he was leading. The portrayal of Navalny himself reached a new low in this stage, with a consistent volume of press describing not just his policies or mistakes, but going further and highlighting interpersonal family issues and attempting to weaken and undermine the integrity of his campaign team by associating them with every negative event or reaction that they could find on the streets. After Navalny's poisoning and admission to a German hospital, however, his image transformed almost overnight. The international publicity and pressure, coupled with the Russian state's apparent hesitance in supporting and facilitating the request for his evacuation to Berlin, meant that a worldwide audience was exposed to what many commentators felt was the unjust and inhumane treatment and behavior of his domestic critics and opponents. Support poured in from across the globe, with fingers being pointed at the suspiciously rapid coverage by Russian media organizations and the seemingly coordinated attempt by officials to deny and disrupt legal and legitimate communication and contact between members of his family and his legal advisors. This resulted in widespread condemnation of both Putin and his administration, as well as the actions of high-ranking members of the federal Russian legal and oversight framework who publicly supported the sham investigation started in Omsk. The chemical nature of the poison involved further inflamed the situation, with special displays of solidarity and support being shown by the EU and NATO in response to what was by now perceived as a state-sponsored act of terrorism under the Chemical Weapons Convention. This sudden 180 in the perception of Navalny, from an inward-looking domestic agitator to a world-renowned and respected democratic icon and figure of freedom against oppression, highlights the sheer impact of this incident.

6.3. Future Prospects

Navalny's impact on the future of Russian politics is still to be seen, but his fresh approach to opposition politics and effective use of social media has certainly changed the status quo. On the one hand, the circumstances surrounding his most recent conviction and the banning of his organizations does suggest that the Putin regime is working harder to rid the country of opposition voices. However, as Navalny's popular video comparing the governance of Russia to a high-profile organized crime group illustrates, he has presented both a viable and exciting alternative and, most importantly, a credible critique of the existing system to the viewing public. This, combined with the public outcry over his alleged poisoning and international scrutiny of the Putin regime, suggests that the future may be capable of huge change under Navalny's leadership. In any case, the significant contribution that the opposition leader is set to make to the political development of Russia has been recognized worldwide - the day after Navalny's arrest in January 2021, the European Union made a formal call for his immediate release, praising his bravery in challenging President Putin's regime. The future of Navalny's political career is very uncertain; on the one hand, his imprisonment and the suppression of his allies may suggest that progress is very difficult under the current regime. However, the rise of the "smart voting" movement combined with the increase in mass protests organized by Navalny's network might just suggest that the political establishment will have to face a real street challenge as a result of his influence. It may also be the case that international condemnations of the Russian government over alleged human rights abuses and illegal suppression of political rights organized his future. Finally, the use of Navalny's image as a political vanguard post-detention certainly presents opportunities for the leader and potential strategies to evade legal and political restrictions, such as the collective leadership of the "Russia of the Future" party and the cessation of the hunger strike of the same name in favor of protests.

PART TWO

ALEXEI NAVALNY'S WIFE
YULIA NAVALNAYA

1. INTRODUCTION

    Navalny, on the other hand, studied law at the Russian State Law Academy in Moscow and graduated in 1998. He then moved to Yale University in the United States and completed his further studies in 2001. After returning to Russia, Navalny started his political activities by joining the Russian United Democratic Party and became one of the youngest members of the political council. Later in 2011, Alexei Navalny became the leader of the "People's Alliance", which is a Russian opposition political party. Even after founding the party, Alexei Navalny faced a series of legal challenges and fraud charges by the Russian government due to expressing his political views. He was also constantly discriminated and not allowed to run in the presidential elections by the government. The importance and impact of Navalny's activism can be identified from the fact that he has declared his intention to stand for the Russian presidency in the 2018 election. This is the first time when Navalny has officially run for public office. In such a critical moment during his political career, the role of his wife becomes crucial. Alexei Navalny's wife, Yulia Navalnaya, has continuously played a significant part in supporting her husband's activism over the years. As a family member of a well-known political activist in Russia, Yulia has personally encountered various struggles and challenges in her life, such as family safety, legal actions and threats from the authorities. Every decision made by Navalny's wife in response to her husband's political crusade brings about serious impacts to their family and personal life. Through understanding the life and role of Alexei Navalny's wife, we can reveal a sense of the importance behind family support and personal sacrifices made by those individuals who are dedicated to political reforms and democratisation in autocratic states.

1.1. Background of Alexei Navalny

Alexei Navalny was born in Butyn, Moscow, on 4th June 1976. He is one of the most vocal critics of Vladimir Putin and has become the leader of the Russian opposition since the 2011 legislative elections. Navalny is an anti-corruption lawyer and the leader of the Russia of the Future party, a national liberal party. He also uses the internet social networking sites to promote the party and to organise demonstrations, protests and meetings. He has been arrested multiple times and received certain sentences, but this has not stopped him from speaking out against the Russian authorities. In fact, his anti-corruption work has exposed the dishonest practices of many members of United Russia, Putin's political party, which undermined the party's and Putin's authority and has made a lot of people angry enough to take him to court dozens of times. He has also led large-scale street protests against Putin. In December 2010, Navalny created the RosPil project, a website aimed at exposing corruption and abuse of government tenders in Russia. On 24th December 2010, the site released several Western Union payment documents suggesting that United Russia politicians were using government money to buy expensive apartments in Moscow for themselves and their families instead of providing housing for war veterans and low-income families, the use for which Russian taxpayers' money was intended. By taking part in street protests, he urged people to join the fight against corruption. In 2013, Navalny ran for Mayor of Moscow as well. He was arrested on 8th July 2013 and taken to court again on 18th July - this time for his involvement in the KirovLes case. However, the court's typist wrote that he was 'held in prison without the instance of shooting a young fountain' as he was released on bail following mass protests in opposition to the Russian authorities once again. Alexei Navalny has made his name as a key opposition figure in Russian politics but has also gained international attention and respect as an anti-corruption champion in the Russian Federation.

1.2. Importance of Alexei Navalny's Wife

The presence of Alexei Navalny's wife in his life and work also contributes to the further development of the activist's opposition movement. After assisting his political activities and moving her family members to a more secure place, Yulia took a more active role in campaigning for her husband. She made many public statements and interviews about the case of her husband and other opposition members in Russia. She also participated in international campaigns and appeals to both raise awareness for the human rights situation in Russia and seek support from the global community. This was particularly important after Alexei Navalny was arrested and imprisoned at different times in connection with his political activities. Yulia has been a very vocal critic of the Russian authorities' crackdown and there have been relentless harassment and persecution against her, including a number of house searches. However, Yulia has still been a very important figure in the opposition movement in Russia. She was involved in organizing and participated in protests and rallies against the current government and in support of a fair and democratic election. Her courage and determination have earned her much respect from other activists and supporters. It is pretty clear now that the current regime sees Yulia as a serious threat to its authority. Over the past few years, Yulia was facing increasing pressure from the authorities. In my memory, there have been countless letters of complaint to the European Court of Human Rights about violations of her rights and freedoms. And these legal battles have placed a lot of pressure on her personally and also her family, particularly her children. Yulia has been forced to take her children out of Russia because she was worried about her safety and her children's safety. She still continues to receive support from her international partners and human rights organizations, with some prominent figures such as Angela Merkel showing personal support for her. Given the international attention over her case, numerous news articles and media coverage have also raised public awareness of her ongoing fight in Russia. Yulia has said in an interview with Deutsche Welle that she hoped with all this international support and attention, her situation and the situation in Russia will improve soon. However, there are still a lot of challenges lying ahead for her and her family. She said that the current regime was trying to use her as a means to put pressure on Alexei. She was concerned that her children would suffer more if her demands and aspirations for a change in the country's policies were heard by the global public and international communities.

2. EARLY LIFE AND EDUCATION

After completing high school, Yulia went on to study in the Moscow International Relations Institute, which is considered one of the leading universities in Russia for social sciences and politics. According to Yulia and her supporters, she was pressured by the university authorities to write a pro-government essay in order to receive a coveted 'red diploma', which acknowledges outstanding academic performance. Furious at the injustice, Yulia wrote a 'powerful feminist' essay and instead received a 'grey diploma', which is seen as a kind of humiliation by scholars. In fact, the colour-coding of diplomas was abandoned many years ago and there is no university regulation to support this belief. However, the story is widely interpreted as symbolizing Yulia's resistance to the authorities and their attempts to persecute independent thinkers and opposition activists. In a blog post, Yulia recounts her university life as 'simple and very hard at the same time'. The post details her modest living conditions, with 'three girls living in a room of 10 square meters', and the 'awful situation' of the Russian higher education system, exemplified by her struggling to find 'any kind of literature' for her studies. Due to her current and future involvement in politics, her educational experience has become a subject of interest for many people. With the apparent difficulties and rigorous academic endeavor Yulia had to undertake, some argue that it could offer an interpretation of her decision to turn to political activism against the status quo. Her political science professor, Aleksandr Kynev, commented that Yulia was 'a very good student' and was 'keeping her eyes open, observing the processes around her'. He told Open Media about his personal worry when he learned that 'one of his best students' is now involved in criminal proceedings against her and she might get arrested at any time due to her civil rights movement. Albeit described as a 'discontents' by some Western media agencies, Yulia's alma mater rejects the notion that the Institute has a political leaning or that it reinforces any discrimination or human rights violation. In a public statement, the Institute maintains that it is 'absolutely inappropriate to make comments on the University's international reputation on the basis of superficial and unfounded interpretations of information'.

2.1. Childhood and Family Background

Her parents, both chemical engineers, were able to provide a comfortable upbringing for their two daughters, managing to "shield" them from the difficulties of everyday life in Russia. Yulia's mother is Roman Catholic, and so Yulia was also baptized in the Catholic tradition. However, Yulia herself is not a practicing Christian; while she acknowledges her mother's faith, she describes herself as an "atheist" who celebrates Christmas and Easter with her mother more as family occasions than religious ones. Her heritage is something she describes with pride (her Polish grandmother's name was Wanda), and it is this part of her background which is now used against her by the more conservative elements of the Russian press. When the rumor began to spread online that she was in a relationship with the Baptist-raised Navalny, they began to be referred to in the press as the "atheist Catholic" and the "religious Baptist". She has made it clear in interviews that she and Alexei share a more secular outlook on faith and see the religious differences in their families as a personal matter.

2.2. Educational Journey

Following completion of secondary school, Yulia went on to study at the Institute of International Economic Relations in Moscow, a prestigious institution that specialized in international relations. This was an exciting time for her as she was living away from home and preparing for her future career. In 1998, she graduated with a first degree in international relations, which was a major achievement. She was delighted and so were her family. She threw herself into her studies, gaining a class medal for her academic successes. With hard work and dedication, she always believed she could do well and this was proven by the fact that she constantly met and exceeded the standards that were expected of her. In fact, one of her lecturers, who was also her dissertation tutor, made the point of saying that "Yulia had an intuitive understanding of material taught, developed the intellectual dependence of issues and presented an objective assessment" - certainly high praise! The dissertation she speaks of was one of several very important pieces of work she completed in her education that focused on a number of different international relations issues. As well as the satisfaction gained from her academic successes, she made many friends from all over Russia and she now looks back on this time in her life very fondly. So university life was indeed an equally important period of her educational and personal development. Both academically and socially, she was more confident and independent. After completing her first degree, she found herself at a bit of a loose end until she began to study for a Ph.D. But during these years, Yulia began to take her position as a leading member of the movement. So first of all, on the completion of her first degree, she began to work as a leading manager of the social democratic youth movement in Russia.

3. RELATIONSHIP WITH ALEXEI NAVALNY

While studying at the Russian State Humanitarian University, Yulia was involved in political campaigning. This was where she met Alexei Navalny, a lawyer and a key opposition figure to Vladimir Putin's regime. They met in 1999 and got married in 2000, and they have two children together. Since starting his political career, Navalny has been arrested on numerous occasions; in 2017, an appeals court in the Kirov regional court in Moscow found him guilty of embezzlement. However, in a very selective move, he was let out on bail so that he could go and take part in the Moscow mayoral elections. But in 2018, the European Court of Human Rights ruled that Navalny's conviction - and the way in which it was made - was in violation of the European Convention on Human Rights, stating that 'independently of the conduct of the accused, the way in which the proceedings in question were conducted, when his right to defend himself was disregarded in a fundamental respect, rendered the overall fairness of the criminal proceedings' verdict open to serious doubt'. Yet despite this, Russian President Vladimir Putin has continued to bar Navalny from standing in elections. Whilst many would assume that a spouse of a political figure would want to see them elected, Yulia's involvement in her husband's work is said to have incited a form of persecution; as part of the embezzlement case that Navalny was found guilty of, both he and his brother Oleg were given three and a half year prison sentences - the day after the conviction, Oleg was taken into custody and

Navalny was said to have been taken into custody in the courthouse, caught on camera by his wife. This was also the case in 2017 when he was taken into custody on charges of illegal protest. On both occasions when Navalny was imprisoned, particularly the three-week period in between the court case and his brother resigning to remainder of his sentence in prison, Yulia publicized the poor conditions in which he was kept in and was very vocal about her husband's plight.

3.1. Meeting and Courtship

They met in the summer of 1999 when they were both studying at the Omsk branch of the Russian State Juridical Academy. At the beginning, Navalny thought that she looked too serious and never smiled. However, it was not long before they became friends and she quickly became the only woman who ever interested him. In the second year of university, they began dating and spent nearly all of their time together. In Anna's third year of university, Navalny decided to ask Anna to marry him and, to his great happiness, she agreed. They married in 2000, a year earlier than was planned in a very modest civil ceremony in Moscow. With all the money that they had between them, they were only able to afford a small flat in the suburbs of Moscow. However, they were both very happy. After Navalny completed his studies at the Academy, he got a job at the Moscow Prosecutors office and Anna found work in a Notary's office. In December 2001, a daughter was born and within a year they were able to move to a comfortable three-roomed apartment in the north of Moscow. In 2015, their pilot project was launched, "RosPil", aimed at judicial in Russia, which Navalny started to show how local citizens could fight corruption and injustice in their hometowns and villages. Anna was one of the first to join this project. She worked extremely hard, spending hours at her computer each day, reading and checking submitted information. She would also travel around Russia, meeting with teams of people who were interested in opening centers and guiding them through the legal registration procedures. When they won the first case, 200,000 roubles was awarded in compensation for corrupt practice in the Kirov Region in favor of her colleague. She continues to play an active role in their anti-corruption programs and her commitment and loyalty was recognized in 2018 when she was presented with an award in the name of Zimin, which is awarded to recognize those individuals who have made a significant contribution to the protection of citizens' rights and civil society in Russia.

3.2. Marriage and Family Life

After the opposition leader Alexei Navalny was arrested, his wife, Yulia, made a public statement on social media: "I am the wife of a man who has been taken hostage by people in power with no legal grounds. But I know that I am right. And when you know that you are right, you should never give up." This statement shows her unyielding support for her husband and his cause. To fully understand the depths of this commitment, one must understand her relationship with Navalny. Navalny and Yulia were married in 2000. The couple has two children, Dasha and Zakhar. They met while studying at the Finance University in Moscow. Navalny was studying securities and exchanges. During her education and later, when she worked for the Moscow State Securities and Exchanges Commission, she went by the name Yulia Navalnaya. In Russian "aya" is used as an ending for surnames to show possession. However, after social media searches could not return any results for "Yulia Navalnaya", she started to change the name to Yulia Navalny to prevent potential future legal issues, which may arise from continuous use of the other surname. Each of the couple married with different surnames and both retain their own original versions up to this date. Yulia participated in Navalny's election campaign and was among the opposition observer team during the 2013 by-elections for the Mayor of Moscow. As her husband's work became more and more politically charged and dangerous, the family faced increasing governmental pressure and violation on their privacy. Navalny and his supporters believe that his recent arrest is politically motivated to stop him from running for the election which may lead to him becoming any form of political power.

3.3. Role in Alexei Navalny's Activism

Yulia has played an important role in supporting her husband's activism in Russia, and the family has faced considerable pressures from the authorities as a result. At the same time, her status as the wife of one of the most prominent political figures in Russia means that she is limited as to how much or what sort of work she can undertake both in terms of her paid work and in terms of her activism, particularly if she were to want to seek refugee status in another country. These are some of the issues that have been raised in media reports by human rights experts, who have noted that the definition of what constitutes persecution under the Refugee Convention and the European Convention on Human Rights includes harm or suffering that is done or is permitted by the authorities with the intention of coercing or punishing a person for that person's political opinion or membership of a particular social group, rather than direct state action. According to a report in The Guardian, one human rights barrister who is an expert in Russian asylum claims has said that there is no specific bar to someone in Yulia's position being recognised as a refugee, provided that she can establish that the harm or suffering she faces from the Russian authorities is for the relevant persecutory purpose, since the interference in her family and private life would not be something that would prevent her from being recognised as a refugee under the Refugee Convention. However, at the same time, the refusal of the Russian authorities to issue her with a needed national passport could also be seen to constitute the persecution of her through the withholding of a legal right, and she would have to consider whether this kind of obstruction by a non-state actor in conjunction with state policies might still constitute a certain kind of persecution. It is understood that she has been refused exit from Russia, and that there is no case currently to answer in relation to her application for asylum in the UK. These reports suggest that the political and legal position she currently finds herself in serves as a stark illustration of the ongoing human rights issues in Russia but also serve to underline her international significance and the potential impact that she could have if she were to be able to continue her work in the UK and seek to exert political pressure on the Russian regime from abroad.

4. SUPPORT AND ADVOCACY

The text begins to narrate how Yulia Navalnaya has supported her husband through trying times and allegations. It talks about how she has chosen to focus on her husband's wellbeing, in response to the recent activities in his life. It states that Mrs. Navalnaya constantly shows strength in adversity and she has a very clear focus to make sure that her husband is released and that justice will prevail. I chose not to include 4.2 and 4.3 in my section because the information was not as relevant and did not flow as well but also because I wanted to stay focused on the key theme of how Yulia Navalnaya has supported her husband through the article. I refer to another point in the essay because it adds to the context in this section and it fits in well by demonstrating another way in which Yulia Navalnaya has shown bravery and resilience. I can look at the second half of the text being included and also consider whether including parts of point 4.2 and 4.3 would be more beneficial to the overall structure. The continuation on the section on support and advocacy seems smooth and then talks about how Yulia Navalnaya has provided public statements and interviews to raise awareness and progress the campaign to free her husband. The phrase "public facing case" adds another layer of understanding in terms of how she manages to balance her private life with her husband and her public desire for justice. It shows that she's considerate of his actions and his image in the public sphere and that she is doing it with the main purpose of releasing her husband. The section ends with another register link phrase "for example". I chose not to include 4.3 because the section was mostly based on the opinions of others and I felt that it didn't flow as well as the main topic of supporting her husband which was outlined in both 4.1 and 4.2. I then reflect back on my chosen points in the conclusion by saying how the many different types of support and advocacy shows Yulia Navalnaya's commitment to justice and perseverance but also that each section of the essay has contributed to forming a more complete analysis of her character and life. The above shows a structured analysis of how I have selected some parts of each section because I feel that it enhances the depth of the discussion and analysis which follows.

4.1. Standing by Alexei Navalny

Yulia Navalnaya has always been at her husband's side both personally and in his political campaigns. In May 2013, when Alexei Navalny was standing trial in the city of Kirov, Yulia stood with him. As Alexei is frequently arrested and faces legal charges, Yulia does whatever she can to support him. In August 2018, when Alexei was imprisoned for breaking the protest law, Yulia walked alongside other protest leaders on the second demonstration against the government's plan to raise the retirement age. In January 2019, when Alexei was arrested just before the rallies, the police forced their way into Yulia's flat early in the morning and he forced her to go with them to the police station and left the children at home. On the day that they got married in 2010, Alexei joked about a potential marriage in prison, considering the prospect that his activism would lead to multiple arrests. Given recent events, this lighthearted commentary seems less humorous. Yulia not only supports Alexei in his campaigns but stands defiantly alongside him facing the same hardships and threats, showing up to protest by his side and fighting legal charges of her own caused by association with him. She describes the allegations of violating public order and assaulting an official levied against her last year during the presidential rallies against Putin's regime as absurd. She said she thinks it is a personal vendetta of one of the police officers against her and she is not afraid. Later in June 2019, when Yulia was fined for demonstrating next to Alexei, she said she will continue to fight for the freedom of Russia. She is persistent in supporting Alexei despite the financial and emotional costs of her activism. Last but not least, Yulia's involvement is not only significant for her but also for her four children and all the supporters in Russia.

45

4.2. Public Statements and Interviews

During the legal battles and subsequent imprisonment of her husband Alexei Navalny, Yulia has communicated repeatedly in the public eye. Particularly since Navalny's re-arrest and imprisonment in January 2021, she has utilized public statements as a platform to both raise awareness of her husband's situation and also to call other countries and human rights organizations to action.

There have been many high-profile interviews with Yulia Navalnaya by major international news outlets. In a Sky News interview conducted on 3 February 2021, Yulia explained that she felt her husband's life was in danger and that he had not only been unjustly imprisoned, but also harmed through a lack of medical care for his various health conditions. She stated that the Russian government should be pressured by foreign governments to provide Alexei with the medical help that she argued he so clearly needs, and she called for European countries to step up and react to the human rights injustices taking place in Russia.

4.3. International Campaigns and Appeals

Her case and her campaign for the release of her husband have received international attention, and there have been a number of campaigns and appeals on his behalf around the world. Perhaps the most high-profile international campaign was the release of Alexei Navalny, which was organized by the chess grandmaster and political activist Garry Kasparov. Thousands signed a petition in support of the campaign, and this was very much seen as a success in terms of raising awareness of the case and applying international pressure on the Russian authorities to release him. This was followed by a similar campaign led by the human rights organization Amnesty International. This was an appeal where people could send a message to Putin and the Federal Security Service in Russia urging them to release Alexei Navalny. It's been reported that around 70,000 appeals were sent, and this was also seen as an effective way in which people in Russia and around the world could express their opposition to the arrest and detention of Navalny in Russia. Another very high-profile international campaign and appeal has been the involvement of the European Court of Human Rights. In early 2021, the Court was called upon to consider a case where Navalny's detention and the charges against him were in breach of the European Convention on Human Rights. The Court's Grand Chamber has since ordered the Russian Government to release Navalny. The problem was that the Russian Government failed to do so and look for some sort of ruling that wasn't actually adhered to by the European Court of Human Rights. However, this case was clearly a significant international appeal and a campaign, and it's one that really reflects the level of international concern about the treatment of Alexei Navalny in Russia under the current regime. Alexei Navalny is a significant global opposition figure; his wife being an important part of that global network, and her case has helped to raise awareness about the significant human rights abuses faced by political prisoners in Russia. Finally, she's also become a symbol of resistance, and this kind of international support for her and for Alexei Navalny clearly demonstrates the level of global solidarity for resistance to the current regime and dictatorship in Russia. She's also received the support of some very influential and high-profile global leaders. For example, in February 2021, she spoke to the members of the Parliamentary Assembly of the Council of Europe, and she was calling for international sanctions against corrupt Russian businessmen. This has involved the freezing of assets that appear in the European Union to have links to the Putin regime, and there have been calls for support for similar measures in the United States. So, therefore, the international campaign has also drawn in the support from quite influential people around the world in a way that is very significant when it comes to public opinion shaping international relations with Russia.

5. CHALLENGES AND PERSECUTION

Despite her significant activism and work in science, Yulia Navalnaya has repeatedly faced challenges and persecution by the Russian authorities. Most notably, the last few years - the run-up to and following the 2021 protests - have seen various kinds of pressure. This has taken the form of numerous administrative cases (and administrative arrests), a series of court cases, and ultimately the removal of her political rights and subsequent 'house arrest' in 2021. Other tactics included attempts by the Russian Investigative Committee to hold her criminally responsible for episodes of mass unrest and the detention and questioning of staff at the Institute of Biochemical Physics. These actions have accelerated a process of what many critics see as the removal of constitutional rights and squeezing of opposition space in Russia. She will now become the best-known figure in a community in which the level of being a public figure is a lived experience - rather than a theory or aspiration. This will create a unique set of material and emotional challenges for herself and her two children - what does this level of scrutiny mean for her research? Or the safety and well-being of her adolescent daughter and teenage son? Can she continue as an advocate for research funding and gender equality within scientific leadership? Trying to balance life under what amounts to an extraordinary form of 'family arrest' with work and raise visibility of the issues facing women in physics will not be a straightforward task.

5.1. Targeted by Russian Authorities

In addition to the smear campaign, Yulia has also been targeted by Russian authorities through legal actions and administrative pressure. In an interview with the BBC, she pointed to the peculiar pattern of cases against her, which often involved seemingly trivial violations. For example, she recounted a case in which she was ordered to perform community service for a charge of disobeying a police officer, when in fact, she had attempted to submit a request to hold a protest earlier and had been told by the policewoman that it was not necessary to file such a request. This kind of petty legal actions and harassment has been a common tactic used in the past by the Russian government against opposition figures and their families. In recent years, Russian authorities have stepped up the pressure on both Yulia and Alexei, as Navalny's influence as a prominent opposition figure continues to grow and he attracts more international attention and support. In February 2014, Yulia and Alexei's apartment was raided by the Russian Investigative Committee in connection with an investigation into the allegedly fraudulent cosmetics company Yves Rocher. It was proposed that Navalny is the mastermind of this embezzlement scheme, while Yulia acted as a co-conspirator in assisting her husband to launder the proceeds. Both of them were charged with major fraud, which carries a maximum sentence of 10 years. Navalny was placed under house arrest a day after the launch of the investigation and subsequently imprisoned for a shorter, three and a half year term. In an interview with the Associated Press, Navalny stated that the legal actions against him and Yulia are politically motivated and means to prevent them from engaging in opposition activities. He also dismissed the notion that his activism has bearing on the charges, pointing to the "absurdity" of putting him under house arrest during investigation for a "completely made up" case. Yulia has consistently denied any wrongdoing in the Yves Rocher case and characterized the allegations against her and Alexei as "complete nonsense". She also stressed that the charges are an attempt to exert psychological pressure and isolate them from public support, and reaffirmed that they will continue their political activities. In the same interview with the BBC, she emphasized the importance to stay active and not to be "scared" by what the government is doing. Both Yulia and Alexei maintain that the charges and investigations are baseless, reflecting the discontent and fear of the authoritarian Putin regime towards a rising, united opposition.

5.2. Legal Battles and Imprisonment

During this period, both Alexei and his wife were convicted for embezzlement under what the European Court of Human Rights found was an unfair trial in 2014. Despite having been sentenced to three and a half years in prison, Alexei ultimately received a suspended sentence. However, his brother was imprisoned for three and a half years. In the context of these legal battles, Alexei's suspended sentence was unexpectedly replaced with an actual prison sentence in December 2014, while he was serving under house arrest as a result of another investigation. He was released on bail a day later, pending an appeal, and he then stood in the race to become the Mayor of Moscow. The convictions for the embezzlement charges were found to have violated the European Convention on Human Rights, and in its judgment of February 2016, the European Court of Human Rights held that Russia had to pay compensation to Alexei and his brother. However, this legal battle also brought political isolation. As a result of the convictions, Alexei became ineligible to stand in elections, and he has often been subjected to other restrictions on his political activity, most notably through re-administration applying rules on restriction for those who have been convicted.

5.3. Impact on Personal Life and Safety

An overwhelming passage about "malice and persecution" which leads to an awful impact on her personal and family life and safety. It is talking about, in addition to the persecution, how the government is targeting Yulia as well in order to punish Alexei. The passage says "despicable act of ordering an unfair home search" which is such an intrusive and devastating experience. It also mentions that the security service, FSB, is using every effort to scare Yulia and Alexei's residents by conducting the home search and confiscating all of their electronic devices, by searching the entire property and accessing all their personal belongings including their children's clothes and toys. It therefore affects Yulia's personal life by illustrating the degree of trauma and humiliation and making her feel unsafe, and also damaging her mental health and wellbeing. The passage emphasizes that the government is using this kind of tactic to try to break the couple down and to prevent Alexei from continuing his political career. It says that "Yulia is the most impressive woman I have ever met. She takes everything in her stride. I think she has more personal strength than anybody I ever knew". This is quite impactful, which indicates the true extent of Yulia's influence on Alexei and as a support to Alexei.

6. ROLE IN OPPOSITION MOVEMENT

Yulia's role in the opposition and the pro-democracy movements in Russia is one that has earned both admiration and ire from different sections of the society and the political class around the world. Yulia has been actively involved in organizing and taking part in protests and rallies meant to sensitize Russians and the international community on the need for an all-inclusive and genuine democratic space in Russia. These include the recent Moscow protests in which the police arrested more than 1,000 protesters and planted her allies cases of money and other incriminating materials. Her admirers regard her as a brave and front line advocate of liberties and freedoms that have been progressively curtailed by Putin's government. Her participation in the protests has been increasing significantly and many of the opposition leader's daily supporters have been circulating petitions calling on her to run for legislative or presidential office. On the other end, the governing elites and their ardent supporters have been seeking to malign and shrink Yulia's influence both within and without the opposition and the civil social circles. In May 2012, just about 12 months before the presidential elections, Alexei was arrested on what many believe to have been trumped up corruption charges. This led to spontaneous protests across the country and in Moscow and it took home the highest number of protesters since the 1993 Russian constitutional crisis. In recent years, the clampdown on basic freedoms in Russia by the establishment has heightened and defiance of the same has become both risky and costly in terms of personal sacrifices and negative backlash from the authorities. Yulia

Tymoshenko, the former prime minister of Ukraine has been quoted in the global media as saying that "In a society where law is disrespected, where there is no freedom, no democracy, even a mere chance of opposing the incumbent government is considered a major political crime".

6.1. Influence on Pro-Democracy Movements

While "Alexei Navalny's Wife" furnishes a wealth of background information on Yulia Navalnaya, her family, upbringing, education, and personal life, the focal and most enthralling aspects of the essay are about Yulia's support for Alexei. Her relationships with friends, family, and crucially, with Alexei, are documented - and it becomes clear she shared his political convictions and has supported him unstintingly in his legal and political battles. Yulia has repeatedly called for the release of her husband, who has been frequently detained by Russian authorities. She has become a major guiding voice in the tenacious resistance to Putin's rule; she has emerged as a powerful figure in the pro-democracy movement. Since 2018, Yulia Navalnaya has repeatedly assumed a prominent position at rallies, protests, and political events across the nation. She has given speeches, participated in campaign marches, and has cooperated and consulted with all major opposition groups. In 2019, her standing as a vocal opponent to Putin was recognized and celebrated when she was presented the "Woman of Courage" award by the U.S. State Department. The award was given in recognition of her struggle to achieve justice for her husband. Before the end of 2020, Yulia was reported as a potential candidate for the 2021 Russian legislative election and could have become a genuine political rival to President Putin. Last November, she advised the U.S. Congress to impose fresh sanctions on Russia to tackle the widespread corruption. This is a massive testament to her increasing influence and the international recognition of her efforts. It's a distinct possibility, even though the essay explores this in the future outlook segment, that she might now lead the country towards a "more principled and stronger path founded on truth and honesty," as she told the Congressional committee.

6.2. Support from Activists and Supporters

When she became more involved in opposing Russian President Vladimir Putin, she found herself the subject of constant surveillance, being followed and watched everywhere she went, often with Alexei and her children. Russian authorities also initiated various legal proceedings against her, mainly on the grounds of her participation in protest activities and events both in Russia and abroad. For example, her name was put on a so-called "stop list", preventing her from traveling out of the country, because of her participation in an unsanctioned street demonstration in the centre of Moscow, during which she was arrested. However, in an interview with CNN in 2018, she expressed defiance against being targeted. She highlighted that it was a retaliation from the authorities to the "peaceful everyday fight" waged by her and her husband against "the regime." Her case was also taken up by human rights groups and organisations. Amnesty International, for instance, designated her as a "prisoner of conscience". This term refers to individuals who have either not committed any crime, but are imprisoned as a direct result of their beliefs or identity, or have been convicted of crimes that did not meet international standards for a fair trial, such as exercising their rights to freedom of expression or assembly. Front Line Defenders also highlighted that her treatment by the government was "part of a trend of clamping down on the work of political activists and human rights defenders by the government." Such campaigns and work by activists and non-governmental organizations around the world have effectively increased pressure and criticism on the Russian authorities. For example, the Finnish ambassador for human rights and Russian non-governmental organization Agora Human Rights Group have both publicly called for her name to be removed from the "stop list". Such international support not only provides her with a form of moral and diplomatic reinforcement, but also shows the flaws and illegitimacy of certain laws and policies that are cruel and unethical.

6.3. Participation in Protests and Rallies

She has also turned her attention to defending political freedoms and human rights in Russia, often participating in protests and rallies alongside Navalny's other supporters. These events are typically orchestrated to push for reforms and to give a public demonstration of the strength of feeling against the Russian authorities. One of the main opposition movements is known as the Democratic Coalition, which champions several progressive causes such as electoral reform, freedom of information, and a diminishment of the influence of Russian corruption on politics. This cross-party group, under the leadership of Navalny, has fielded political candidates and objected to Moscow city legislature election procedures. In the lead up to this major election during 2018, Yulia's participation in events such as the 'March of the mothers' and 'Stop the Tsar's procession' drew widespread attention from both domestic and international media. In the latter rally - so named in protest of the alleged intent of Putin to stand for his hundredth combined term as either prime minister or president – Yulia Kalezheva directly addressed the crowd in the place of her husband and spoke of her reasons for taking part in the event. She has said in separate interviews that she hopes the progressive cause will have an effect in future elections and that her efforts may serve as a lightning rod for change. The fact that Kalezheva has made speeches and publicly voiced her opinions on candidates for the presidency suggests she is becoming a more formidable potential opposition figure to the establishment powers. The general public seems to be receptive to the calls for change, with footage and images emerging of large crowds during these rallies. As of yet, there have been no reprisals or actions taken against Yulia for her involvement in the protests, either by legal authorities or by political opponents. These rallies remain an important tool and a means of transmitting a message to the government about the necessity for progressive reforms in Russia's democratic systems and, in particular, to present a united front against the rule of the United Russia party led by President Putin. She also used her Twitter account, which boasts over 18,000 followers, to share images and experiences from the rallies and to encourage more people to attend such events to 'make necessary change'. These kinds of direct actions and positive reactions to her involvement are evidence that her public support and capability as a figurehead for protest is growing, which could indicate that in the years to come, she will quickly rise to prominence as a significant opposition voice in Russia.

7. INTERNATIONAL RECOGNITION AND SUPPORT

In the UK, the Foreign Minister Dominic Raab said that the investigation on Navalny's condition is essential and must be fully supported. The European Court of Human Rights has already ordered the Russian government to release Navalny from his detention after his legal representatives lodged an application last week. This came a day after the 44-year-old anti-corruption campaigner, who was detained shortly after his return to Moscow, urged tens of thousands of supporters to take to the street via a video released by his aid while he is in remand.

In Germany, a nation where Navalny was airlifted to for medical treatment and where it was later confirmed that he was poisoned with Novichok nerve agent, the President Frank-Walter Steinmeier and Chancellor Angela Merkel visited Navalny in hospital. Merkel described this incident as "attempted murder using nerve agent" and demanded Russia to "explain itself in full". The call to investigate and hold the Putin's government accountable has gained traction after Navalny has recovered and returned to Russia in January 2021, especially in view of the ongoing protests and the mass arrest of over 11,000 people in two days after his return.

After Navalny was poisoned in August 2020, significant international support for Yulia grew. She has persistently reiterated her belief that the Russian government, led by Putin, tried to knowingly kill her husband, but he survived "by fluke" and not due to the administration's intention of preserving his life. This stance has drawn attention from global leaders and helped to raise awareness of the corruption and human rights abuse in Russia.

7.1. Solidarity From Global Leaders

The unlawful arrest and subsequent sentencing of Alexei Navalny was met with global outrage and protests. In response to his imprisonment, there was no shortage of condemnatory statements from world leaders. Countries in the European Union, such as Germany, France, and Sweden, as well as the United States, all called for Navalny's immediate release. EU officials repeatedly described the arrest as politically motivated. The obstruction and suppression of lawful assembly and freedom of speech led to mass protests in Russia and further condemnation from abroad: the UK, Canada, the European Union, and the United States criticized the Russian authorities' violence towards peaceful protesters and journalists and voiced their support in favor of upholding democratic principles. Perhaps most notably, President Biden not only condemned the treatment of Navalny, saying that he had been targeted for revealing 'corruption that exists' as well as calling his treatment 'totally unfair', he also imposed sanctions on Russia. These sanctions, which included targeting the Nord Stream 2 pipeline, were the most significant action taken against Russia by any global leader. They bolstered both the legitimacy of Navalny's cause and the view of him as a significant opposition figure. The impact of such support is likely to be felt not only on a diplomatic level but in directing further attention and solidarity towards Navalny. One of the protest campaigns emerged on social media with the hashtag #StandWithNavalny, promoted by his colleagues and thousands of international supporters. This international attention and condemnation are likely to be instrumental in sustaining the pressure on the Russian government and President Vladimir Putin; indeed, Russian officials have been notably dismissive and confrontational in their responses to criticisms from abroad. Such endorsements from global powers bring attention to not just the specific case of Navalny but the broader necessity for improved human rights and revision of oppressive legislation in Russia.

These expressions of solidarity could go beyond Navalny's case to bolster the political opposition and general calls for reform in response to his anti-corruption advocacy. The coordinated reactions of world leaders may serve to embolden and coalesce.

7.2. Human Rights Organizations' Response

For instance, Amnesty International filed several cases on behalf of Alexei Navalny and his allies. These include the case against the house arrests of Alexei Navalny, his brother Oleg Navalny, and the case against the prohibition for Alexei Navalny and his supporters to organize rallies and meetings. The European Court of Human Rights accepted the first case and on 16 February 2017 ruled that the Navalny brothers' house arrest in the criminal prosecutions gave rise to a violation of the European Convention due to "arbitrary and manifestly unreasonable" house arrest. The Court also acknowledged the complaints of Mr. Alexei Navalny. On 15 September 2020, the European Court of Human Rights accepted his complaint as a priority. As such, any decision made by the Russian Central Electoral Commission on whether he is ineligible for the upcoming elections due to the suspended sentence would be immediately regarded by the Council of Europe as a provisional measure of the European Court of Human Rights. According to the director of Amnesty International and other prominent figures in similar institutions, Navalnayas v. Russia is a test case reflecting the ability of the European Court to ensure effective justice in Russia for a prominent government critic and his family members. However, despite the progress, there are still various ways in which the Russian authorities try to jeopardize the efforts of Navalnys and their counselors. For example, the decision made by the Central Electoral Commission can be appealed against at the Supreme Court, which means a prolonged legal process in Russia and an uncertain future. This is especially the case given that the situation has been exacerbated by the outbreak of the COVID-19 pandemic, which led to significant backlogs in the Russian judicial system. Also, evidence in recent years shows an increasing reluctance to comply with the European Court of Human Rights' decisions, whereby the Russian authorities often intentionally delay the execution of judgments or refuse to take any measures to comply with them. It remains to be seen how the European Union, the Council of Europe, and other international institutions would react if the Russian government deliberately ignores any interim measure issued by the

European Court. However, the provisionality of such international measures and the uncertainty of the final decision by the European Court will continue to be used by Russian authorities to suppress the activities and ambitions of their political opponents.

7.3. Media Coverage and Public Opinion

Among the various topics and incidents associated with Alexei Navalny and his family, media outlets have showcased a genuine interest in Yulia Navalnaya's life over the years. Many articles and news segments in Russia and the international sphere have been dedicated to analyzing and investigating Yulia's life, such as the quality of her marriage or her work life, as well as her political preferences and activities within and outside of Russia. For example, it is largely speculated that Yulia, who has kept working and maintained a family life despite her husband's runs for presidency and his various incarcerations, would have a different opinion on political matters. There are many news stories that focus on growing opposition support and the influence of political spouses in Russia.

In fact, a number of authors describe Yulia as "the Russian first lady in waiting" and an example of a new, westernized, 'protest' lifestyle among the educated middle classes. This constant attention of the public, delivered by the media coverage of her daily life and her privacy being altered by the public, may also explain why Yulia is known to avoid journalists and paparazzi to the biggest extent possible, with Anastasia Vasilyeva, the head doctor of the Alliance of Doctors and a close family friend of the Navalny, even stating in a number of interviews that "Yulia is a very private person. She is not seeking publicity but does all the campaigns and the kids and everything."

Despite the importance that the media coverage would suggest and the potential detrimental effect to a woman who aims to build a private life and exercise her human rights, particularly her freedom of expression and privacy, not much work has been done in Yulia regarding a potential 'invasion of privacy' and protection under human rights law. It is rather ironic that the lack of articles and discussions about the breach of privacy in Yulia's life actually serves to empower the recognition of a breach, since it is louder proving the creation of a 'political image' through aggregated information and systematic intrusion upon one's personal sphere over a 'celebrity' lifestyle and personal choices.

8. FUTURE OUTLOOK

Sobol's future looks bright, as she continues to be a rising star in the opposition. In September 2020, she was nominated among the top three female politicians in the "Beautiful Power" category of the annual "Top 100 Most Influential Russian Women" award. Despite the growing pressures and challenges she faces in her personal and professional life, Sobol is determined to make a change. She continues to work as a lawyer and politician, in addition to her role in Navalny's Anti-Corruption Fund. More importantly, she is currently the head of the regional political party office and plans to participate in the upcoming parliamentary elections in 2021. If she decides to run as a candidate in the elections, Sobol will likely apply her nomination immunity right as a candidate (similar to Navalny's right) to avoid potential prosecution and, if elected as a Member of Parliament, she will gain parliamentary immunity. And this immunity would give her additional protection against any politically-motivated lawsuits and sanctions from the Russian government. With the global outcry following Navalny's imprisonment and the protests happening in the country, Sobol's work and efforts in pushing for more international sanctions against the Russian government may potentially gain more attention and resources for the opposition. On the other hand, given the uncertain political outlook and the ever-increasing suppression, the important role that Sobol plays in the opposition and her growing influence will likely cause the authorities to step up their attempts to weaken her. Over the past few months, there have been reports of increasing harassment and threats against Sobol and her family. On 27

December 2020, Sobol's father and brother were taken into police custody without any justified reason, for "questioning". This is a clear attempt to put pressure on her and her family and to divert her focus from the activism and the preparation for the elections. However, authorities are not only challenging her politically, they are also attempting to discredit her reputation. On 1 January 2021, Sobol was fined for participating in the "unauthorized" protest in July 2019 and she was accused of insult and physically harming the Russian Investigative Committee officer who unjustly arrested her during the protest. This is a typical tactic for the authorities to fabricate criminal accusations and to create obstacles in her political career.

8.1. Continuing Activism and Advocacy

After Alexei's imprisonment in December 2014, Yulia has continued to work and support her husband despite constant threats and intimidation. She has also taken an active role in the Russian opposition movement and is one of the leaders of the "League of Voters." This is a platform that encourages public political activity and is aimed at raising public awareness about elections and the political environment in Russia. In her work with the "League of Voters," she has faced numerous attempts to disrupt and discredit her work. In 2016, an unlawful "inspection" was carried out, during which, as the European Court of Human Rights would later find, her rights under Article 8 of the European Convention on Human Rights, which protects privacy and family life, and Article 11, which protects freedom of association and assembly. This led to a court case, which she won, demonstrating her commitment and success in using legal avenues and international institutions to fight against the Russian authorities.

8.2. Potential Impact on Russian Politics

There is a lack of clear evidence that Yulia will actually become an active player in Russian politics. However, her husband's status as a prominent opposition leader who may have been potentially poisoned by the government with Novichok now has created a very good ground for Yulia to actually become another hope for the Russian opposition movement. Two months after arriving in Germany, Yulia Navalnaya has taken on a more political role, recording a video address earlier this October in which she makes an emotional appeal to Russian citizens, urging them to participate in a three-day protest movement. In my opinion, if Alexei Navalny is not able to fully recover, Yulia Navalnaya will receive and require more help from the Western countries and human rights activists, which will provide a fertile ground for her to step into Russian politics. In addition, Yulia quickly gained the reputation as a de facto gutsy and resolute opposition figure in Russia after she flew to Germany to retrieve her husband from the verge of death and fight the "big guy" in the Russian government, namely Putin. She dauntlessly disquiets the safety threats and constantly stood up to Russian authorities by fiercely criticizing the lack of government action against poisoning her husband. Some political analysts put forward that with the dissenting momentum build-up with the alleged poisoning of her husband—which eventually draws international attention and peaceful protests across the whole Russian Federation—this will accommodate an opportunity for Yulia to delve into politics actively. So overall, we can be reasonably optimistic about Yulia's future. However, I personally believe it will largely depend on either Alexei Navalny's recovery progresses and the Russian government's next move.

8.3. Personal and Professional Aspirations

Yulia has some personal and professional aspirations that she would like to work towards. For instance, she is very interested in charity work and would like to be involved in organizing and furthering it. She has always enjoyed handing out food and clothes to the homeless and would like to be able to do something more organized so that she can really make a difference to people's lives. She would also like to join a think tank and write opinion pieces on various issues. She already writes for the women's section of the People's Democratic Union and she would like to be able to write for a more prestigious or well-known publication, in order to spread the message of the opposition to a wider audience. She has had pieces published in the Moscow Times and the Guardian, but she is not allowed to own her own publishing company, so for the time being she is living with her grandmother's, Olga Lutskaya, who is the founder and head of the Lutskaya Foundation. This is the foundation where Yulia met Ivan Zhdanov, who works there, and, as of December, Yulia's brother also works there as a translator. Yulia, however, may need to step up her role in the organization during 2021, as her sister and Mrs. Lutskaya herself become progressively more unwell with Parkinson's Disease. Mrs. Lutskaya had until recently been entirely independent of care and had visited the EU Parliament to petition against electoral fraud; it is a great worry for Yulia and her family that the foundation be able to continue to run even if she is unable to continue working. Mrs. Lutskaya is planning to apply for a research grant from Europe in order that her research can be protected and the foundation can continue during 2021, but failing any successful grant applications, Yulia and Olga are concerned that they may need to consider research into setting up a charitable incorporated organization. Yulia is passionate about children's rights and her lasting declaration to the Save the Children Charity which focused on child mortality within Russia has raised over £2,000. Yulia recently had a publication accepted by the Lund Human Rights Research Hub and Vol 6, No 2 (2020). The paper used Kantian ethical theory to qualify and highlight insufficiencies in the UN Declaration of Human Rights in its application to the political imprisonment of figureheads of opposition movements.

PART THREE

CHILDREN OF ALEXEI NAVALNY

1. BACKGROUND

A family of well-educated professionals, the parents advocated for their children's development. Navalny's mother reportedly recognized him as a highly capable, talented child. While the Navalnys' candidates for the State Duma never won on the party list, Anatoly once stood in the municipal election and Lyudmila joined the Federal Drug Control Service as a consultant. Though not in a position of a politician, Anatoly was a member of a mass political movement and his piece about problems of the Russian postal service was published in a news outlet that "supports the Communist Party of the Russian Federation" when he was required to comment on the "administrative abuse" by his supervisor. By analyzing the relationship between his parents and politics, a report by CNN suggested that Navalny's disenchantment with the practices of public officials might stem from his father's experience and the structure of the family, which encouraged political discussions.

Navalny was born in Butyn, a town located in the Odintsovsky District of the Moscow Oblast, Russia, in 1976. His father, Anatoly Navalny, served as a conscript in the Soviet Army before working as a postal official and then a businessman. He is currently a vice rector at the Russian State Social University in Moscow. His mother, Lyudmila Navalnaya, graduated from the Moscow State Linguistic University and worked in the pharmaceutical industry, including managing distribution for major national and international drug companies. She also owns a country house and an apartment near Moscow. Navalny has a brother, Oleg, who is older by two years, as well as a younger sister. His whole family moved from Butyn to the large residential complex in the district of Kommunarka in the late 1980s and registered as residents in the Soviet House.

1.1. Early Life

Navalny was born in the capital of Russia, Moscow, on 4th June 1976. He was brought up in a family of intellectuals - his father was an army officer while his mother was employed as an economist. This middle-class family had a comfortable lifestyle. Navalny's father served in the air force of the USSR before retiring in the year 1990. His parents were well-educated, open-minded, and did not have any strong political views. His father was a man of principle who always encouraged his son to be competitive. As a child, Navalny was quiet and spent much time reading. He was very obedient and a good student at school. He showed a great interest in extracurricular activities offered by the school. In a television interview, his mother described him as a curious and persistent character from an early age. This curiosity and eagerness to learn were further enhanced with the arrival of his younger brother, Oleg. They had a close bond and spent a lot of time playing and studying together. Navalny always made an effort to help his younger brother in studies.

1.2. Education

After finishing school in 1994, he had to choose a place to continue his studies. He preferred to go to a different city and become a student of the Moscow State Institute of International Relations - one of the most prestigious places in Russia. The choice of the specific faculty was not that simple. Apart from becoming an advocate, a student could have been educated for a diplomat or a journalist. He chose to study international law and soon realized that the decision was correct. Being a freshman, he and several students organized a small group, which supported democratic values and human rights in Russia. Later, the group evolved into the 'Yabloko' - one of the most significant democratic parties in the 1993-1996 period of the Russian history. During the years in the Institute, his political orientation was forming as well as his value as an activist, lawyer and a public figure. In 1998 Alexei finished the Institute and got a diploma with honors. Then he made another crucial decision - to defend a thesis. After successful presentation of the final work, he acquired a scientific degree and became a candidate of sciences in international law. This was one of the first significant achievements of Alexei. He was offered to stay in the Institute, however, he preferred practical work. It is always hard to make a choice - to pass away from calm and measured student's life and start to act without any guarantees. He decided to make a progress in legal sphere and went to practice to a quite famous lawyer. From the first days of job Alexei was involved in defending of human rights and political corpse. Such practice has completely shaped his future as a politician. He was sure that it is impossible to work and develop in the corrupted system, so he referred to human rights activities. It was a troublesome period for Alexei and all the civil society activists. In the conditions of suppression from authorities and lacking of impartiality of the upper courts, he applied to the European Human Rights Court concerning violative imprisonment. It is a thorny path from the local district court to the international body and it took Alexei more than ten years to bring the case to a successful final. However, this process seemed to be a help guide for many children and adults who, just like Alexei, happened to be in the situation, when the basic human rights and equality under the law are violated.

2. FAMILY

Alexei Navalny was born in 1976, in Butyn, a town in the Moscow region. His father, Anatoly Navalny, was a military officer, and his mother, Lyudmila Navalnaya, was a housewife. Navalny spent his childhood in Obninsk, where he moved with his parents when he was still a small child. Both of his parents are alive and well today. His father served in the Soviet Army for many years and then worked at a factory, whereas his mother was always a typical housewife, taking care of the household and children. Navalny has a brother, Oleg, who is two years older than him. Navalny often says that his family is the reason why he gradually became more and more interested in politics, even though no one else in the family has ever been involved in anything like that. Navalny wrote about his family in his blog and in numerous interviews and social videos. He shared some quite intimate details of his family life, described the philosophy of life that his parents instilled in him, and talked about his relationships with his wife and kids. Navalny truly appreciates the support and understanding that his family provides, and it is clear that family plays a very important role in his life. His supporters often mention the fact that he managed to maintain such a strong and loving family while being involved in such a risky and dynamic activity, and it certainly adds to the positive image that Navalny has. However, at the same time, the media and some of the critics often use his family for their own purposes, starting rumors and attacks on his family members, and even trying to involve them in some political events or affairs. Navalny's public persona and private life are often the subject of discussion and political manipulation in Russian media, and his family members are not safe from this kind of attention, either. This draws even more attention to his family life and creates additional pressure and responsibility.

2.1. Parents

Navalny's father, Anatoliy Navalnyy, is from Dzhankoy, Crimea. He has a PhD in metallurgical engineering and currently works as Deputy Director at the Russian postal service. His mother, Lyudmila Ivanovna, is from Kursk. She graduated from the Medical Institute in 1984 and now is a pediatrician in a city hospital. Alexei Navalnyy is not an only child in his family. He also has a younger brother, Oleg. Oleg is lesser known to the public and prefers not to be involved in his brother's political career. He was born in 1986 and graduated from Bauman Moscow State Technical University. He is a qualified specialist in information technologies and remote system controllers but his actual job is unknown to the public. His wife, Viktoria, was given power of attorney over his personal affairs and family's guardianship for his daughter after Alexei Navalnyy was imprisoned. It was said that she sent a message for help after Alexei was poisoned by Novichok but she has never been able to confirm her power of attorney because her appearance was unclear in an interview video. So there is a question raised by the public on how the application of power of attorney and guardianship by Viktoria Navalnaya can sustain after Alexei Navalnyy was poisoned by a deadly toxin. Last but not least, there are two lovely children in Alexei Navalnyy's family. His son is named Zahar and daughter is named Daria. It is said that Zahar is very talented in sports and he studies in the First Moscow Cadet Corps. On the other hand, Kirov Medical Academy in Saint Petersburg has already given a place to Daria as a university student by the presidential quota in 2020. It is quite rare and only a few famous people's families and children can directly enter universities in Russia in this way. In an interview by a British journalist, Alexei Navalny explained that his daughter was admitted to the university representing political moves by Putin to give a more democratic and humanitarian look in the public eye after he had been poisoned. There is no doubt that Alexei Navalnyy has become a protective and loving father to his children. However, apart from individual happiness, Alexei Navalnyy has been concerning the collective interests in his country and never stopped moving forward.

2.2. Siblings

Aleksey Navalny's siblings include Oleg and Ivan. Oleg is the middle child and he was born in 1980. As he was just 3 years old when Aleksey was born, they have always been very close. During an interview, Oleg spoke about the love and admiration he holds for his brother and his children refer to Aleksey as Uncle Lyosha, a shortened, affectionate form of the name Aleksey. Ivan is the youngest child of the Navalny family. There is a 13-year age gap between Ivan and Aleksey and as a result, Ivan did not grow up in the same family environment as his siblings. He has left his family in Moscow and moved to the US for postgraduate studies. When asked about his brother's imprisonment, Ivan expressed his anger and frustration. He stated that his brother criticizes the Russian government and nothing more. Ivan maintains that he does not understand the reason why his brother was imprisoned and he believes that it is a way to silence independent politicians like his brother. Both brothers also share their sibling's political views. They consider Aleksey as a driven person and they also trust their brother to fulfill their mission. However, they do not believe that they will be involved in the political issues anytime soon. Aleksey has admired his younger brother Ivan. He has described him as an inquisitive, ambitious, and intelligent young man. Aleksey has also spoken about the important role Ivan has played in his anti-corruption work. He said that he heavily relies on Ivan's support and knowledge of technology for his political blog. Ivan also helps advocate for technological solutions to help public participation in fighting against corruption. Aleksey mentioned that he is excited to see how his brother will develop himself as a political force and make inroads into areas of academia. However, he has also commented that Ivan must have a thick skin if he is to be involved essentially in Russian public life.

3. PERSONAL LIFE

Navalny met his wife, Yulia, in college and the two got married in 2000. They share two children together, a daughter named Daria and a son named Zakhar. In 2008, Alexei and Yulia welcomed their first child, Daria. Three years later, Zakhar was born in 2011. In addition to her role as a mother, Yulia is also active in her husband's professional life. She is an economist by trade and often helps with her husband's businesses. For example, Yulia has aided Alexei with his campaign finances and has served as the chief financial officer for the Fund for the Fight Against Corruption. As previously mentioned, Navalny's family is under constant public scrutiny and they are often the targets of smear campaigns and harassment. Unfortunately, his children have also felt the effects of this pressure. His oldest child, Daria, had to change schools at the age of 12 because classmates verbally abused her due to her father's activism. In an emotional post shared on social media, Navalny expressed the pain and frustration he felt when he realized that his daughter was facing this kind of adversity. He explained that he recognized the importance of continuing his fight against political injustices in the country and that it was a hardship his family had to bear, but that knowledge did not ease his pain. He expressed how proud he was of Daria for her strength and resilience. This information perfectly underlines the struggles that Navalny and his family face on a daily basis due to his political activism and the Russian government's treatment of them.

3.1. Relationships

Alexei Navalny married his wife, Yulia, in 2000. Their daughter, Daria, was born in 2001 and their son, Zakhar, was born in 2008. Navalny and his family lived peacefully in Obninsk, where he worked as a lawyer, before they moved to Moscow in 2009. After a series of small disagreements with the Kremlin and the uncovering of various corrupt practices, things came to a head when Navalny made his name by exposing a 500bn rouble fraud in 2010. The government's response was to place him under house arrest and to remove his right to use the internet, preventing him from working. This event, and the arbitrary and biased way in which it was carried out, further damaged the relationship he had with those in power, making it impossible for him to have his claims of electoral fraud properly investigated and resulting in the events of 2011 and 2012. However, Navalny's arrest served as the lightning rod for widespread anti-Putin protests; thousands took to the streets in cities across Russia, and 70,000 signed a petition demanding his release. Since then, Navalny's relationship with the Russian state has continued to worsen and has been typified by crackdowns on free speech and widespread repression, culminating in the arrest at the airport in January 2021, which in turn led to the nationwide protests discussed in the introduction. He continues to be persecuted greatly as a result of the government's hostility: his wife has been arrested, his organizations have been suppressed, and his supporters have been disbarred from standing in the upcoming election. This kind of sustained and widespread suppression of political freedoms is a significant concern to the international community. On 11th February 2021, the European Court of Human Rights ruled that violence against Navalny's supporters and their subsequent arrest were breaches of international law and that the Russian state should now take the necessary steps to protect them.

3.2. Hobbies and Interests

Navalny is a strong supporter of the Russian soccer team Spartak Moscow. He often goes to their matches and follows their progress very keenly. On the other hand, Navalny is a critic of the government's extensive financial support for his team, which he views as inappropriate and corrupt. He also writes on his blog that his ideal holiday would be a sunny day in the forests near Moscow, picking mushrooms and having a barbecue with his family. He enjoys this very traditional Russian pastime and the laid-back atmosphere it brings. Today, this appeal to traditional activities and Russian culture could partially explain his popularity amongst some sections of society, particularly the older generations. Moreover, his enjoyment of quiet, family time in the serene Russian wildernesses may also explain his firm opposition to President Vladimir Putin's economic policies, which he sees as continually damaging Russian society and family life. Also, this simple, traditional way of life is directly contrasted to the high-spending and sometimes ostentatious habits of some of the political elite around Putin and Navalny's main political opponents.

4. CAREER

Alexei Navalny started his career in political activism after joining the liberal Yabloko party in 2000. He later changed his party affiliation to United Russia in 2004. Navalny quickly became disillusioned with the party's leadership and its ideological shift to the right. In 2007, he was expelled from the party and began to focus on his anti-corruption activities. In 2011, just a few months after Putin's party, United Russia, had suffered big losses in local elections, Navalny attracted national attention when he started blogging about large-scale corruption in state-controlled companies. So great was his influence that he was arrested in December 2011 and sentenced to 15 days in prison for defying a political protest on the eve of Putin's inauguration for a third presidential term. The European Court of Human Rights ruled that Navalny's right to a fair trial had been violated in relation to the prosecution over the use of public property for commercial gain when he was found guilty in 2017. Navalny has often been described as the leader of Putin's "opposition" but he does not associate himself with the term. He established the Anti-Corruption Foundation in 2011 and Russia of the Future in 2012. The former has published a large volume of material online, claiming to expose corruption among Russia's highest-ranking politicians, political parties, and state corporations. He has also authored various legislative initiatives. For example, Russian citizens can now sign up to a website and vote to start a public debate on proposed legislation if they get 100,000 signatures. In 2013, Navalny stood for election for Mayor of Moscow and he attracted large, youthful crowds to his campaign rallies. Navalny came second with

27%. In recent years, he has called publicly for Russia to adopt a "visa-ban system" and he has closed down his Facebook account, claiming that the Russian authorities submitted demands to him about removing material from the site.

4.1. Professional Achievements

It is not until he got older and started his career that he began to achieve great success and recognition internationally. Having obtained a degree in finance and securities at the Finance Academy, Alexei went on to get a second degree in law from the Russian State Juridical Academy. This was a turning point in his career. In 2011, he became the chief of the party's anti-corruption activities. He led a powerful and effective campaign in which members of the party would carry out orchestrated rallies of several thousand demonstrators, in which poster after poster made allegations of high-level corruption linked with members of the Russian government and the United Russia party, including Vladimir Putin and Dmitry Medvedev. His anti-corruption organization had begun fighting for the liberation of Russia from this deadweight of persistent and pervasive corruption. As a result, he became the face of the Russian political opposition both at home and abroad and, recognizing his high public profile, Alexei chose to break off his work at the legislature and turn his focus on his external activities. He founded the Russia of the Future party, aiming to create a fair and functioning political system for his country, but his application to the Ministry of Justice to recognize the party was illegally denied, resulting in legal action being taken. His law activities have been significant also. In 2018 and 2019, he was seen to act for several voters in the Russian presidential election, challenging the election held on 18 March 2018 on the basis of the disqualification of the candidate. In 2019, he acted for two voters who challenged the election to the Moscow City Duma and an act of the incumbent. He continues to undertake public interest litigation in Russia, particularly against the electoral authorities. Specifically, he brought a number of challenges against the decision of the Moscow City Electoral Commission to refuse to register him as a candidate for the post of Deputy of the Moscow City Duma in 2019. His pioneer work has led him to big success including a number of domestic and international awards - he was consistently awarded a Tier 1 ranking by The Legal 500; an internationally recognized guide for law firms and lawyers - from 2017 to 2019. This is particularly significant as this ranking is said to be based on merit and demonstrable evidence of the ability and expertise. From the year 2017 up to now, Alexei has been recommended by The Legal 500 as a lawyer, which is a huge recognition for his work in the field. He was also named as the Best Lawyer in the field of information technology and intellectual property. He also managed to get several foreign awards including an arbitration award by the London Court of International Arbitration and an award of judicial review in the High Court of England. In September 2019, Alexei officially became a partner of the top law firm in Moscow at the dispute resolution practice. His team, being led by him, was recognized with a top-tier ranking by The Legal 500 for dispute resolution in Russia. His team again was recognized by The Legal 500 in July 2017 as the best Russian practice in the area of information technology.

4.2. Political Involvement

Navalny's political career began in 2000, when he was a first-year student at the Russian State Law Academy in Moscow. He helped organize students for "Yabloko," a liberal political party. From 2000 to 2002, he was active in the party's youth wing. Navalny's ties to the liberal "Yabloko" party soon weakened. When they nominated an alternative candidate for the 2003 Moscow City Duma elections, he supported the National Democratic Party instead. However, Navalny soon became critical of the National Democrats and began to describe himself as a "nationalist democrat." In June 2001, Navalny established the "Alumni Brotherly Help" (Bratja Po Pomoschi) organization, which he ran until 2007. In 2008, he started to work for the public stock company "Transneft" as a pro bono adviser. However, this was not to last and in February 2009, Navalny wrote an article exposing a legal case of corruption against "Transneft" senior officials. This was his first major public investigation. He started a blog in March 2008. The theme of his articles varied from political issues to the problems of daily life. However, Navalny's most influential work came in December 2010, when he launched a public project against corruption, "Rospil." This appealed to a wider spectrum of Russian society and strengthened Navalny's position as a political figure. He attracted widespread media coverage for alleging embezzlement by Russian officials with regard to state procurements. This culminated in the successful registration of "Rospil" as an NGO by Navalny in March 2011, although it has since been targeted under the foreign agents law. This notoriety brought from his anti-corruption activity had the effect of heightening the profile of his theories about political reform. His creation of the Anti-corruption Foundation in 2011 combined with rising public support set the conflict with Russian officialdom in a political rather than in a purely juristic plane. His arrest in December 2011 quickly became controversial, as it was seen as a repressive tactic used by the government to silence an increasingly popular figure in the opposition movement. With Navalny's relatively short political career, as a result of his anti-corruption activity, he has been targeted with a number of defamation lawsuits from Russian officials. Navalny and his allies consider these lawsuits as a form of legal harassment and a violation of his right to freedom of speech and public interest.

5. CONTROVERSIES

There have been numerous other legal challenges and controversies that Navalny has faced over the years, ranging from multiple short-term arrests for participating in unauthorized political demonstrations to more serious cases such as the Yves Rocher fraud case. Whilst Navalny claims all of these accusations are politically motivated, there is no doubt that such legal issues have had an impact on his work, as well as serving to maintain a narrative of hostility against his character.

Although the Russian authorities have not succeeded in destroying or banning the Anti-Corruption Foundation, the authorities have targeted other Navalny-associated groups. For example, in 2019 the Justice Ministry declared the Anti-Corruption Foundation as a "foreign agent", causing it to be subject to additional monitoring and limitations on its activities. This has been widely denounced as an attempt to discredit Navalny and his work in the eyes of the public.

Navalny's political career has been marked by various legal challenges and controversies. One of the most widely publicized legal issues that he has faced dates back to 2009, when Alexei Navalny was sued by the then Moscow City Council deputy, Vladimir Samsonov, for defamation. Navalny had accused the politician of being involved in corruption on his blog, leading Samsonov to sue for damages. Despite the fact that the European Court of Human Rights found in 2018 that Navalny's right to a fair trial had been violated in the case, he was ordered to pay around 450,000 rubles in damages to Samsonov. Navalny has appealed to Russia's Supreme Court over the decision.

5.1. Legal Issues

The charges and legal action taken against Navalny are varied. For example, the European Court of Human Rights denounced the 2014 Yves Rocher case against Navalny, calling it "arbitrary and manifestly unreasonable". In other cases, such as the KirovLes case, Navalny has been found guilty in lower courts, but not before the decision is contradicted by a higher court. At the same time, just days after he was barred from running against Putin, Navalny was arrested and his brother, Oleg Navalny, was imprisoned for 3 and a half years. This example of guilt by association is consistent with the idea that many criminal proceedings against Navalny are politically motivated. Alongside his menagerie of criminal allegations, Navalny has also been a target of legal barriers and intimidation specifically designed to impede his political career. For instance, in April, a Moscow court fined him 300,000 Russian rubles for organising unsanctioned rallies. This legal penalty was mirrored by a threefold increase in the frequency of temporary arrests that Navalny was subjected to between 2016 and 2017, as well as the seizure of parts of his campaign office's IT equipment. All these legal issues show that Alexei Navalny has been continuously harassed and arbitrarily detained and prosecuted. The en masse arrests of his supporters during the 2019 presidential election, a campaign that he was barred from running in anyway, display the extent to which systemic tactics of legal interference are used to undermine his cause. In short, the legal issues section of "Children of Alexei Navalny" serves to exemplify the seriousness and breadth of resistance encountered by him in his fight for a free and fair Russia.

5.2. Media Attention

The media plays a major role in publicizing not only countries but public figures too. Alexei Navalny, because of his various anti-corruption investigations and his continuous protests, has always been in the limelight of the national and international media. The leading pro-government and state-owned TV channels and other news outlets, which have only a few viewers, heavily went against Alexei Navalny during the rising of his "mass-protests" on March 26. Mr. Navalny took the unusual step of using a video game to public innocence over the decision to jail him for 15 days after a series of street protests. He directed his followers to reach a high score on a retro-style game mocking the activities of the riot police. Also, he used to oppose the media and the government's accusations on him by providing proof and evidence to cases and using his YouTube channel to reveal the government's corruption stories. Also, Mr. Navalny used the media to get support from other countries and to get the sympathy of the international public. For example, when he was taken seriously ill, he was hospitalized in Siberia and his life was saved by an air ambulance where he was transferred to Berlin and they have diagnosed that he was poisoned by a type of nerve agent called Novichok. He and his supporters accused President Vladimir Putin of being responsible for his poisoning and to take his life and he had a chance of receiving good medical care to save his life. There are different types of media in Russia, such as newspapers, magazines, TV, radio, online, and social media. The government and the President's office have the most control on media, especially the TV channels are the main source of information for the public and most of them are working in favor of Putin's presidency. The content of this section reflects the theoretical results to show what existing literature suggests about the impact of media in a particular context. The knowledge from this could be important for a media production unit if successful campaigners or journalists start using the media. Because of the advanced technology, the media is providing up-to-the-minute information to the public. So, as a result of that, public perception could be changed by how the media frames, places, and presents stories about political issues and by how the public is talking about said issues online.

6. IMPACT

After years of activities and political campaigns, quite many people know him in the street. Everybody's assuming him to be some kind of very famous politician, but not many understand who he is and what he is actually doing. The politicians knew quite well who Alexei is because his name appears in all the political legislation papers that have been issued in the 21st century. Shell companies, corrupt government officers, rigged election systems... he brought all these official misconducts to the public and displayed the evidence very well in his blogs and social media. He also participated in all kinds of average Russians' lives: he filed hundreds of complaints to the European Human Rights Court on behalf of Russian citizens against various types of official misconducts, he led public demonstrations for free and fair elections, he registered the opposition camp, a new political party, and started a series of public protests and demonstrations. He helped to wake up the middle class in Russia to the crisis of human rights in the 21st century, when the protesters' reaction to the government is edible food for the riot police to beat them harder. He is the only lawyer who could achieve such a victory in the European Human Rights Court that formed the case law of the court for all European citizens. When there's official media propaganda to criticize him, he successfully sued the government in the European Human Rights Court, which constitutionally protected his rights of privacy and free speech. Whenever government officers publish 'authoritative expos', all the information would be disclaimed by stating "the controversial person whom the officer is talking about refused to comment on the relevant facts and no one could reach him for his own story." However, what he actually replied to the so-called 'corruption expos' is "should anybody can reach the author? I would like him to address the fact how ridiculous his conclusion is." And the government still has no budget on the official TV or newspaper to produce such a 'manual for practical defamation'. The nine successful appeals out of ten rejection decisions on different cases of criminal prosecution, ranging from theft to the offense of disobeying police command and protest management, is the best demonstration of how corrupted the police is. Yet the authorities still initiate another two or three investigations every year. He is now serving a sentence of 3.5 years by the fraud verdict, but... his popularity increased overwhelmingly in Russia. People start to realize that they probably should not believe the media who criticize Alexei, should not affirm themselves being apolitical, and should not trust the official jurisprudence anymore. I believe that you could find out how influential Alexei may change the global political landscape if he is a free man.

6.1. Influence on Politics

Alexei Navalny has made a significant impact on politics in Russia. His first major political challenge came in 2011, when he was appointed to the leadership of the Russian Democratic Party Yabloko in Moscow. However, in the same year, the party's leading body decided to remove all three leaders, which led Navalny to leave the party. Afterwards, he helped to found a new political movement called the People's Alliance, which aimed to unite the opposition and develop a long-term socioeconomic program for the country. During the Moscow mayoral elections in 2013, Navalny's campaign for Moscow mayor represented a significant watershed for the development of the opposition in Russia: a newcomer to electoral politics rapidly built a sophisticated campaign based on the newest communication and organization methods. Ultimately, the results of the protests in 2011 gave a major boost to the opposition and Navalny's leadership strengths because they signaled an end to Putin's political hegemony. The protests proved that a great mobilization of the population was possible, and millions of Russians realized that the secure world Putin had created in Russia was an illusion. The power of the internet in politics has become a major aspect of the development of the Russian opposition - and the government's strategies to counter the impact of online political activity. The growth of political blogging represented in some ways a new phenomenon within Russian politics: cyber-activism and cyber-politics. From 2011-12, Navalny became one of the central figures in the initiation of mass street protests against electoral fraud and rallies against Putin's regime. The internet was a hugely significant tool that helped to amplify the messages of the political opposition in Russia. The power of new technologies and social media has been seen worldwide in many recent political events, from the Arab Spring to President Obama's successful digital media campaign. However, within a few days of the start of Navalny's trial for embezzlement in the city of Kirov, he was found guilty and received a 5-year suspended sentence, and his brother was sent to prison. This not only stopped Navalny from his developing political destiny by putting him behind bars but also represented a move by the Kremlin to remove a serious contender to Putin's reign. The fact that the sentencing in the Kirov case was seen to be a grotesque abuse of the legal process and a transparent effort to silence Navalny laid bare the increasing authoritarianism and unwillingness of the government in Russia to engage in even the most basic form of democratic practice. The image of the smiling figure of Vladimir Putin embracing a party of delegates from the United Russia National Congress on November 27, 2013, which was uploaded to the internet, was a sign of how much the Russian government disregarded the opinion of the rest of the world in its attempts to maintain the status quo in Russian politics. The caption of the photo reads, "most of the room was filled with United Russia Party Delegates, and they all stood up and applauded the president in a 10-minute standing ovation." This suggests that the modern-day opposition movements in Russia represented by people like Navalny will face not only a stubborn and authoritarian state regime but also a population that is largely disinterested and despondent with the prospect of political change.

6.2. Public Perception

Navalny's work has attracted criticism from the mainstream media. He has been linked to a variety of increasingly bizarre and almost certainly fallacious conspiracy theories. His perceived influence has also developed over time. After his name became significant, many of his investigations would be tied back to a contrived semblance of hidden political motivation. For instance, some media outlets suggested that he published his accusations against the government not in the interest of justice, but rather to start a career in politics. Some argue that Navalny's habit of protesting outside the State Duma produced the suspicious regularity of mass demonstrations. This, some said, created the appearance of a remarkable public response and hence exaggerated his noteworthiness, when in reality it was the result of orchestrated unrest. However, whilst the Russian government has labelled him a populist without a significant following, Navalny's campaign during the 2013 Moscow mayoral elections noticeably increased both his perceived popularity and general media mentions. Furthermore, political motivation is increasingly hard to justify, especially given the fact that all of his accusations were publicly accessible on his blog, where he was not in need of further support to bolster his viewership. This is not to say that criticism remains baseless, but rather it reflects the divergence in public opinion regarding Navalny's work, which geopolitical analysts have argued has become much more polarised in the modern day. Creative Commons Sharealike

7. FUTURE PLANS

After finishing his suspended sentence in 2018, Navalny suggested creating a new campaign across Russia. His initial steps in this campaign included establishing campaign offices in regions across Russia, 300 in total, and intending to flood the country with volunteers. The purpose of this campaign is to put pressure on the Kremlin, engage those disenchanted with the current system, and prepare an infrastructure for a presidential campaign, he told the Financial Times. In order to do concerted work in the regions, many campaigns would be focused locally. By May, all offices were either opened or in the process of opening, Navalny said. He was disqualified from running after his campaign's legal entity was declared a "foreign agent," but the campaign continued as a basis for future planned activity. The "Foreign Agents" Act was introduced in 2012 and it required all NGOs that receive foreign funding and deemed to be engaged in political activities to register and declare themselves as "foreign agents." However, the scope of the Act was expanded since it was introduced. Now it covers any organization engaged in vaguely defined political activities and receiving any amount of funding from abroad. Furthermore, there has been a campaign of targeted inspections of prominent NGOs by Russian state authorities in the past 6 years, including Amnesty International, Human Rights Watch and Transparency International. Amnesty International went to court and successfully challenged in the Supreme Court the legality of the Ministry of Justice's decision to list it as a "foreign agent." However, Navalny's has not been successful and it has been forced to dissolve due to its financial situation. He has tried to call for a nationwide protests and cross-Moscow demonstrations but he has been arrested and detained by the police several times last year, including a detainment of 30 days in August for the calls for the unauthorized protests, according to the New York Times. Also, his brother's companies are under attack. In the trials, there is no evidence for the criminal actions were taken by Oleg Navalny and Navalny himself. This has gained global media attention. Children of Alexei Navalny have often been mentioned in global media. His eldest son, who studies at Yale University, wrote quite a few blog posts to criticize Putin's domestic and foreign policy, particularly for the annexation of Crimea, according to the Moscow Times. He also wrote an open letter raising concern for the safety of his father and the deterioration of the political situation in Russia, the Moscow Times reported, expressing the view that "his dad is not just a politician, [he is] an opposition leader-- who is seen as a big threat to the current system." Also, a few global media outlets, including BBC and The Guardian, have reported that children of Alexei Navalny have taken part in various protests defending their father. His younger brother, Oleg Navalny, has been involved in all the trials with Alexei Navalny and suffered detention, yet still keeps criticizing the Russian justice system until now. Last year, a number of world leaders called for the release of the opposition leader Alexei Navalny following his arrest, including Chancellor Angela Merkel of Germany, President Emmanuel Macron of France, and the British Foreign Secretary Boris Johnson, according to The Independent. They all expressed concern about the proportionality of the police's application of force. However, President Putin disregarded the criticism and called the Western reaction "a part of the Western efforts to contain Russia's development," The Independent reported.

7.1. Goals and Aspirations

Navalny wants more than just personal success – he wants Russia to be a better place. Navalny lists "taking part in the fight against corruption" as one of his "key achievements" and says that his goals include "changing the current political situation in Russia" and "becoming a well-known figure in the opposition." It is likely that Navalny would continue to work in public service if he could. However, he is worried that if he succeeded in his defamation case, his political career could be cut short. Defendants in defamation cases in Russia can face prison sentences of up to five years, and this could bar him from running for office. It remains to be seen how these aims will be affected by his ongoing legal cases and potential future imprisonment. Despite these challenges, he is still hopeful about the future – in an Instagram post from 2019, he wrote that "I'm absolutely confident that my children will live in a Russia where everyone is equal before the law." His long-term ambition is to run for president, but for now, it looks like his main focus will be on getting through the legal difficulties that lie ahead. He is fiercely critical of the current government and recently accused the Russian President, Vladimir Putin, of creating an "imitation democracy." This sharp criticism, along with his frequent investigations into alleged corruption, has provoked angry responses from pro-government media, and he has faced challenges in mobilizing voters. However, his protests have still gained traction – in recent years, he has been imprisoned for periods of weeks or months at a time for his support of political protests. He has also repeatedly been the victim of assault; most notably, in 2016, he was attacked by a group of three men who sprayed a green antiseptic chemical in his face. Although the attack initially damaged his vision, he has since made a partial recovery. Nonetheless, his hope for the future is that these issues will be resolved and that he will have the opportunity to bring about the change he desires.

7.2. Potential Challenges

Political activism can pose significant challenges for an individual's family. Family members, especially underage children, can be subject to certain difficulties due to the fame and public exposure of their parent. Alexei Navalny's children are likely to face similar issues as Navalny's political career progresses. One potential challenge may be the attention and disruptions to their daily life from admirers or from the media. As Navalny's popularity increases, so will the attention on his family. This could lead to fans or journalists consistently monitoring his children, which will become a major concern for their safety and well-being. In addition, as Navalny's children grow up in an environment where their father is constantly under public scrutiny, this may influence their perception of what normal family relationships should be like. They may become accustomed to lack of privacy, which is often associated with high-profile political figures. Protective measures such as supervision and heavy policing of personal information may distance them from the real world and from forming genuine friendships and developing their own identity. Last but not least, there may be potential legal challenges in guaranteeing their right to a free, happy childhood, away from extreme public and media interest. If this aspect of their life is heavily interfered with and they are restricted from living a normal childhood, then it may be that their rights, under Russian law or within the context of the European Convention of Human Rights, could have been violated. This might lead to legal proceedings or intervention from social services to remove them from that situation, as a matter of protecting their welfare. All of these challenges would be emotionally and psychologically damaging for Navalny's children to grow up under and we want to avoid the situation where their life would be adversely hijacked by the political convictions of their father. Therefore, the issue on children protection as a potential challenge for Navalny's family should not be underestimated.

PART FOUR

DEATH OF ALEXEI NAVALNY

1. BACKGROUND

Although Alexei Navalny was relatively unknown in Russia until 2008, when he began to use social media, his life before that point was also marked by the themes of anti-corruption work and the "liberal agenda" in the country. Navalny was born in June 1976, in Butyn, a small town in Russia, about 20 miles outside of Moscow. In 1980, his family moved to Moscow, as his father, who was an official in the Soviet army, was transferred to the capital. Navalny studied Law at the Peoples' Friendship University of Russia in Moscow, where he first became involved in the liberal and anti-corruption youth groups. After graduating, Navalny began working as a lawyer. He later opened his own business, a small corporate law firm, which specialized in dispute resolution. Navalny's activism really began in 2008, before the parliamentary elections in Russia. He bought a few shares in the major Russian state-owned oil company, Rosneft, and traveled to the United States to obtain evidence for a lawsuit.

1.1. Early Life and Activism

Navalny was born in Butyn, near Moscow, in 1976. His parents were well educated; his father served in the Russian Army and his mother was a university graduate. In the early 1990s, Navalny moved to Moscow to study law at the People's Friendship University. While there, Navalny joined the Union of Right Forces, a liberal political party, and quickly became known for his speeches at demonstrations and his activism challenging the ruling government. After graduating in 1998, Navalny continued to rise through the ranks of the Union of Right Forces, serving as head of the local branch of the youth wing and taking part in the party's conflict with Putin's United Russia party over control of the Moscow city Duma. However, his political career really began to take off when, in 2011, he began investigating corruption schemes in the United Russia party and Russian corporations. This resulted in a number of mass protests across the country, with Navalny being a leading figure in the opposition movement. This also brought him into direct conflict with Putin and his associates, with Navalny being tried and imprisoned numerous times over charges which he and the European Court of Human Rights have deemed to be politically motivated.

1.2. Political Career

Alexei Navalny's political career took off in 2010 when he started the Party of Progress. He has since built up a reputation for being both a staunch critic of Putin and corruption in Russia. Navalny has consistently been in and out of jail for his criticism, and in 2017 was found guilty of embezzlement and given a five-year suspended sentence - he claimed this was politically motivated. Despite this, he has always been a leading figure in the opposition movement. Navalny has been well known in Russia and internationally for his anti-corruption videos about the ruling party "United Russia" and about Putin himself. The most famous of these is a film investigating the then Prime Minister Dmitry Medvedev's links to corrupt practices and politicians in Russia. Navalny tried running for office in 2013 and put himself forward to be mayor of Moscow. However, his bid was unsuccessful because the Kremlin-backed candidate won.

2. POISONING INCIDENT

On 20 August 2020, Navalny fell into a coma after having tea at Tomsk Bogashevo airport and then took off on the flight to Moscow. According to his spokesperson Kira Yarmish, some time later, in the plane, he was poisoned. As it was a serious condition, on the initiative of the pilot, the plane almost immediately landed in Omsk. It is said that the ambulance took him to a hospital straight away and within an hour after his collapse on the plane he had been hospitalized. Alexei felt bad already in the morning, it was difficult for him to come to life after 4 hours of sleep and he drank a cup of tea about 30 minutes before the departure but he became much worse after the tea. The Omsk medical professionals immediately started acting in accordance with the international standards and resuscitated Alexey. His state was evaluated as grave; pulmonary edema, metabolic disturbances and a sharp drop of blood sugar were diagnosed. Even though the wife and the press secretary requested his transfer to Germany, the Russian medics had been assuring that there was no obstacle for such a transfer but his condition didn't allow it. At this point Russian doctors claimed that his state was stabilized and he had been taken out of medically induced coma, Alexei however was still connected to the ventilator. At the same time the Charite hospital in Berlin, where a lot of post-Soviet politicians and public activists used to be treated, declared its readiness to accept Alexei. On 22 August a medical team from "Cinema for peace" fund arrived in Omsk. The experts were supposed to transport Alexei to Berlin and therefore establish what kind of transport was medically suitable. On 22 August

in the evening, the medical team of "Cinema for Peace" fund transported Alexei in a medical aircraft out of Russia to Germany for the continuation of the treatment. They had arrived in Russia on the day before and now they are first arranging the transport and taking him to Berlin. The situation has received widespread international attention. There have been calls for an official investigation, with several European countries offering to help. In the meantime more and more details are revealed. In particular, it is reported that the baggage convoy with the parcel of water had departed from the hotel "Xander" along with the police and shortly afterwards the head of the criminal investigation department for road accident inspections of the Russian Federation across the Tomsk region had ordered to examine the hotel for finding for the pieces of evidence in relation to the offenses stipulated in the Criminal code. Also, one of the stories packed up by the German RBB TV program is that the aircraft with Alexei had arrived in Omsk very early in the morning and then the team of the employees of the hospital and his colleagues immediately started opening the back door of the aircraft, so the scene vividly looked as if they were escaping with him. Yet this symbol of tragedy and hope is not going to finish soon.

2.1. Initial Symptoms

On August 20, 2020, Alexei Navalny became violently ill during a flight from Tomsk, Siberia to Moscow. His symptoms began when the plane took off and continued to worsen throughout the journey. According to one eyewitness, who was a passenger on the same flight, Navalny could be heard groaning and screaming in the airplane toilet. Upon arrival in Moscow, the plane made an emergency landing and Navalny was taken to the hospital. This eyewitness account and the timeline of Navalny's symptoms were covered by various media and were compared with statements made by the Russian authorities and the flight company. German government sources have said that Navalny's symptoms were first exhibited in the airplane rather than after he had left the airport. This information was used as evidence in legal proceedings in Russia and in the context of political discussions concerning the ill-fated journey of the opponent of the current Russian government. In response to the medical situation on the airplane, a spokesperson for the flight company stated that no passengers had requested medical assistance during the flight. However, the eyewitness's report and other media coverage did not support this statement, and many pointed out the fact that the flight attendants had not paid any attention to Navalny's medical state during the journey. In a news briefing after the emergency landing in Omsk, the first doctor who treated Navalny initially said that no traces of any poisons had been found in his blood, urine, or stomach. He has also suggested that the politician might have been affected by a high level of glucose in his system. However, Navalny's personal doctor and the Russian government permitted his medical evacuation to Germany after the German government offered assistance. This contradicts the public statements made by Russian authorities and medical professionals consulted by the Omsk hospital, which repeatedly said that Navalny was too ill to be moved. Navalny's family and supporters believed that there might have been a political motivation behind the delay in allowing access to further medical examinations and treatment in Germany. This incident has sparked global media coverage, international condemnation, and diplomatic tensions between Western countries and Russia.

2.2. Hospitalization and Treatment

Finally, after a lot of pressure from his family and a specific request from the Chancellor, Angela Merkel, Alexei Navalny is allowed to be transferred to the Berlin-based hospital from Russia for further treatment. Chancellor Merkel's office and other European leaders have called for an investigation into the incident. Kremlin spokesman Dmitry Peskov has wished Navalny a "speedy recovery" and said that "in this case, the best doctors should be involved in determining the diagnosis" for treatment in Germany. On 22nd August, Navalny is brought to Germany. A few days later, on 24th August, the hospital says in a statement that the team at Charite have examined Mr. Navalny and the clinical findings indicate poisoning. Then, the hospital revealed that the 44-year-old is in an induced coma and is placed on mechanical ventilation. Also, the statement confirmed that the medical results indicate poisoning with a substance from the cholinesterase inhibitor group. Cholinesterase inhibitors are chemicals that can slow down the breakdown of the neurotransmitter acetylcholine, and when it is working properly, the neurotransmitter acetylcholine is responsible for controlling functions such as muscles and memory. Although the statement did not state the specific substance involved, it's still an important lead for identifying the toxin.

2.3. International Response

The case of Navalny prompted international response as a result of the activist's influence at home and abroad. Tensions between Russia and the West were already high and the poisoning of this crucial opposition voice only served to escalate matters. Germany was the first country to publicly announce that Navalny had been poisoned with Novichok, a military-grade nerve agent, and suggested that it was a targeted attack being carried out on someone within the jurisdiction of the Russian state. Angela Merkel led the calls for a response and there was a clamour within the European Union for the controversial Nord Stream 2 pipeline - that would allow Russia to bypass Ukraine and Poland when supplying gas to EU member states - to be scrapped. This would be a significant embarrassment to Putin and an economic blow to Russia itself. Indeed, even before the investigation was concluded into Navalny's condition, some of his supporters were raising the possibility that he would be deliberately poisoned in order to silence his vocal criticism of the Russian president. The pressure on the Russian state grew further still when French and Swedish laboratories independently verified the findings of their German counterparts with regards to the substance that had been used.

Despite this, the official Russian line remained largely dismissive of the prospects of a foreign-led investigation that Putin has described as "nothing but hot air" on state television. The Russian ambassador to the UK, Andrei Kelin, said that he was "devastated" when the UK and the Americans also insisted on sanctioning Russia further. He insisted that open disclosure from the German authorities and the provision of evidence by the British government would surely allow the Russians to properly investigate the situation their own way. But the approach of the domestic and international communities had varied very little since the start of the episode and, for the first few weeks of the investigation, it had appeared as though Kremlin critics around the globe had significant cause for concern. Navalny had to be transported to Germany for better medical care after a group of demonstrators went against airport directives, swarming the ambulance where first aid paramedics were attending to him in Omsk. This incident grew into a call for wider, peaceful rallies, which were met with a surprisingly passive police response for the first few days. However, there were claims that officers were authorizing a controlled opposition in

Russian media debate; it was suggested that state news outline the locations of counter-protests and effectively "forced" airing to ensure a minimum turn-out that could be portrayed as representing the popular angle of the status quo.

3. INVESTIGATION

Navalny's poisoning and rushed to a hospital in Siberia. The following day, he was transferred to a hospital in Berlin due to the severity of his condition, and tests confirmed the presence of a cholinesterase inhibitor in his system. This substance prevents the human nervous system from breaking down nerve agents, leading to symptoms such as vomiting, sweating, and muscle weakness which may also suppress the respiratory system, potentially leading to death. The Russian government has denied any involvement in the poisoning, and Putin himself has suggested that the opposition may have poisoned Navalny in order to frame the regime. However, the use of a Novichok agent - a type of nerve agent developed by the Soviet Union and used in the Salisbury poisonings of 2018 - has raised suspicions, particularly in the light of Russia's previous involvement in such incidents. Furthermore, other political figures and critics of the ruling United Russia party have since become ill or died in unexplained circumstances, leading to speculation that the Kremlin is carrying out targeted poisonings in order to eliminate opposition. Despite the denial of access to the investigation by Russian authorities, various independent investigations have been carried out across the world. Investigations in France and Sweden have corroborated the German conclusion that Navalny was poisoned with Novichok, and in the European Parliament, representatives have voted to condemn the attack and call for the suspension of Nord Stream 2, a gas pipeline project between Russia and Germany. Alexei Navalny died at the age of 44 on 20th August 2020. The announcement of his death came whilst he was still in a coma; in a Moscow hospital, hang on to life by a thread.

3.1. Russian Government's Stance

The Russian government has consistently denied any involvement in the poisoning of Alexei Navalny, referring to the incident as a purely internal affair and dismissing suggestions of foreign intervention. Several leading officials publicly expressed skepticism regarding the poisoning and resented what they perceived as interference by Western nations that had offered assistance to Navalny. Foreign Minister Sergey Lavrov accused Germany - where Navalny had been transferred and treated - of failing to provide the Russian authorities with medical information and preliminary test results. President Vladimir Putin himself appeared uncharacteristically exasperated when questioned about the affair, asserting that it was not being talked about out of genuine concern for Navalny himself but rather as an excuse to place sanctions on Russia. Throughout September 2020, Putin's schedule was repeatedly interrupted by demonstrations across Russia in support of Navalny and a full investigation into the poisoning; according to the President's Press Secretary, the chief aim of the protests was to 'disgustingly pressure the authorities by creating certain conditions for dialogue with the so-called leaders of the process'. The Russian government further made demands upon foreign powers and institutions to respect the country's legal sovereignty and to engage with appropriate channels according to international law when responding to Navalny's poisoning. In late October, members of the Organization for the Prohibition of Chemical Weapons - which Russia maintains had acted unlawfully in allowing samples to be taken out of the country through arrangements with Germany - met to discuss progress on investigations; there was no significant statement issued or concrete change in the ongoing international dispute.

3.2. Independent Investigations

A number of independent investigations into Navalny's poisoning using Novichok took place. The first of these was carried out by the "Bellingcat" organisation, a group of investigative journalists. This investigation claimed that members of the Russian Federal Security

Service (FSB) were involved in tracking Navalny's movements in the years leading up to the attempt on his life. The investigation also featured a phone call. This phone call was made by a member of the FSB to a chemical weapons expert shortly after the attempt on Navalny's life. The Bellingcat team managed to obtain a recording of this phone call, in which the FSB member discusses Navalny's suspected poisoning and requests that no traces of 'biomarkers' are discovered in his body. Such a request would hinder the investigative process. The phone call supports the Bellingcat conclusion that state involvement in the poisoning of Alexei Navalny is strongly indicated.

3.3. Accusations and Denials

A number of accusations have been made in relation to Navalny's poisoning, with various parties offering different perspectives. Some of the key accusations and the subsequent denials are outlined below. Firstly, it was suggested that Navalny may have been poisoned at a location outside of Russia, with some commentators pointing to the possibility of the Novichok nerve agent being administered in Germany. However, this suggestion was strongly denied by the Russian authorities, with the Prosecutor-General's office indicating that there was no data to support this. Secondly, it was suggested by the Russian government that Navalny may have poisoned himself, either intentionally or accidentally, in order to embarrass the authorities. However, Navalny has described such a belief as "so insulting". In fact, no criminal investigation has been opened into potential suicide attempts by Navalny and his team have dismissed the notion that he accidentally poisoned himself, highlighting the fact that Russian authorities prevented Navalny from being transferred to a specialist medical team in Europe for over a day. This, in turn, has been used to support the theory that the Russian authorities deliberately delayed his transfer in order to allow the poison to leave his system, casting doubt on the narrative that Navalny himself was responsible for the incident. The Russian government has also faced accusations that it sought to cover up the poisoning of Navalny by not opening a criminal investigation, and attempting to prevent the involvement of the international community. The European Court of Human Rights has since ruled that Russia must conduct an investigation into the poisoning of Navalny, and that his life was in danger whilst he was on Russian soil. However, the Russian government has dismissed this ruling, insisting that it was made on the basis of evidence that was not available at the time. Instead, Russia has indicated that it will attempt to contest the ruling and has criticized the use of international law in imposing the decision. This reflects a wider criticism of the Russian government and President Putin, who has faced accusations of failing to uphold human rights and the rule of law, both in Russia and within the international community.

4. NAVALNY'S DEATH

On 11th May, 2021, Navalny's spokeswoman announced that he was "dying" while in Russian prison due to being denied access to a doctor. On 12th May, 2021, Navalny's lawyers said his health was deteriorating and he appeared almost "emaciated". Russian authorities and different prison officials have always denied that Navalny's health was in such a life-threatening situation. The Russian ambassador was summoned in Ireland after neighbors of Navalny raised the alarm over his deteriorating health. Later that night, European politicians and MEPs started to call on the EU to press Russia to allow captive hunger striker Alexei Navalny access to proper medical care. Angela Merkel, the German chancellor, expressed concerns on Alexei Navalny and saying that she and Vladimir Putin could meet if required over Navalny's health. On April 20th, 2021, Alexei Navalny's doctor Anastasia Vasilieva announced that test results had shown that Navalny's condition was potentially life-threatening and that a high potassium level had been detected and that Navalny could suffer a heart attack "any minute". However, two days later, she was formally accused of spreading banned protest images online and she was put under house arrest until 14th June, 2021. On 23rd May, 2021, Anastasia Vasilieva fled from Russia in order to continue her work and to avoid legal consequences. On August 24th, 2021, Navalny's press secretary announced on his social media accounts that a rapid deterioration in his health: "This latest symptom says we are experiencing a third wave of the attack." On 9th September, 2021, three laboratories across Europe confirmed that Alexei Navalny was poisoned by a nerve agent that could originate from a specific complex of chemical weapon - part of Russia's chemical warfare. The European Union imposed sanctions, targeting key development tools and technology for Russia's oil and gas industry that is estimated to be worth $5.66 trillion. This would significantly impact Russia's long-term energy potential and target the area exploited by Nord Stream 2 project, a gas pipeline project, where Putin's close associate and Kremlin's 2nd most powerful person, Dmitry Kozak, is heavily involved. On 12th September, 2021, Navalny's spokeswoman announced that an acute gain-of-function disorder at eye-nerve junctions was detected and that the risk of going blind in "one or both eyes. On 17th September, 2021, Navalny's lawyers reported that the prison has "significantly changed" the light situation inside his cell: the prison's searchlight has been set to shine directly at Alexei's bed and with the maximum brightness during the night". On 23rd September, 2021, White House press secretary Jen Psaki tweeted that the United States is deeply concerned about the fears for Alexei Navalny's health in Russia and "he must be allowed to be medically evaluated independent and unconditionally". On 25th September, 2021, Alexei Navalny was transferred to an unknown district hospital for prisoners despite objections by his doctors. On 29th September, 2021, Anastasia Vasilieva, who fled from Russia and has transitioned to be his personal doctor, announced that his condition has partially stabilized despite leaching weight. His lawyers also reported that prison visits and access to him have been denied and that Russia faced independent legal challenge in international court in Strasbourg over the treatment of Alexei Navalny. On 7th October, 2021, it was announced that Navalny's daughter applied to be granted asylum in the United States. On 15th October, 2021, the EU have issued a statement demanding Russia to "unconditionally release Alexei Navalny and to ensure his safety and health" and that the EU "held the right to take adequate action in response to a breach against fundamental rights and for assaulting opposition leader Alexei Navalny". On 17th December, 2021, the prison service announced that his name was removed from the prisoners register - indicating that Navalny was dead in the Russian penal colony. However, the press secretary waited until 21st December, 2021, to formally release the information.

4.1. Confirmation and Announcement

After Navalny was moved to Berlin, Germany, with a specific end goal to get treatment, his situation stayed basic and the possibility of his survival was viewed as disillusioning and practically incomprehensible. This conviction was visible in the open articulations made by Russian authorities; for example, the representative of President Putin suggested Navalny's serious condition as a PR trick and even expressed that never in his life had he at any point heard in regards to Navalny. This naturally set up the foundation for the progressing between condition. In actuality, independent doctors who have broke down the tests given by Mr. Navalny's family have affirmed that the traces of a destructive nerve specialist from the Novichok amass were found in the consequences of Mr. Navalny's studies. These discoveries from free specialists are generally thought to leave next to zero space for a fractional or full disavowal on the confirmation and the ensuing charged accusations and comments from the Russian government. All the more imperatively, after an extensive time of examination and recoup, Mr. Navalny stays oblivious and was come back to Germany, where he was recouped and woke up. This means the outside examination will proceed and the Russian government, in spite of its continuing disavowals and accusations against outside countries that connected with the case, for example, Germany and United Kingdom, is currently under noteworthy universal weight. The Russia specialists have two times reached those must audit the record the final product of which is to expel him from the enlistment as a result of the conviction and capture having started against Mr. Navalny. Such news was plainly essential. First of all, it demonstrated that the clinical tests directed by the independent specialists were trusted by specialists, including cancer-causing agent specialists or toxicologists. Then again, the way that Mr. Navalny's condition has been developed adequately in the wake of his come back to awareness to enable him to formally apply for chosen as President to Russia has established his direction. This application as of late went under the concentration and there are progressions, including the progressing arrangements for setting up his managerial type of political association with a view on taking an intrigue in future races.

4.2. Public Reaction

In addition to the criminal cases to which Navalny and his allies are accused, the arrests, raids, and internet limitations for the opposition, including his wife, Yulia, and the barred candidates, it is important to develop long-term policies and strategies to combat political risk. On the same date, i.e., 48 hours before his closing hours,

Kirov court sentenced Alexey Navalny to 3.5 years in prison but suspended his imprisonment due to the general amnesty because of his family status. However, such a decision remains to be rocked by the public since all the allegations against Navalny are mainly invalid and groundless. It is believed that such an unfair treatment from the court would never have stopped him from seeking justice for this unfairness suffered by the general public, in particular. This personal opinion is believed to reflect and stimulate what might be actually the truth. On the other hand, most of the citizens in Russia are in view of that the political environment is moving towards a more direktdemokrati, in which the political votes from the citizens would become more and more prominent. However, it is not useful to pursue this route at present, in particular to the Kremlin. This is because the 'Putin system' gives the governors a great deal of power such as the right to appoint the upper chamber of Parliament. Therefore, governors only 'need to keep the support of the weaker lower house to have total control of the legislative progress'. On balance, to effectively combat the region's political risk, defined as the probability that the political status quo was likely to change, considerable changes should be not only simply procedural_cumulative or revolutionary but also critically substantial. At the same time, the influence of the international society should not be neglected. Cognitive such as massive propaganda could be adopted to raise awareness of the social problem in Russia, and this may stimulate pressure for the Russian government to change. Also, the Waste and Drinking Water treatment case (C-124/03) has demonstrated that a successful litigant could be a potent force for change. Similarly, if the opposition groups lodged a judicial review to scrutinize the legality of setbacks, changes in the political systems could be possible.

4.3. Funeral and Memorial Services

On June 5, 2014, Lyudmila Alekseyeva passed away in a hospital in western Germany (one of the moderation messages to a friend after creating a fake account). A number of funeral services organized by his family, friends, and fellow activists accompanied Navalny's death. The first one took place in Berlin. The mourning ceremony to honor the memory of Lyudmila Mikhailovna Alekseyeva, a human rights activist and the head of the Moscow Helsinki Group, was held in Maloyaroslavets in the afternoon - burial. Lyudmila Alekseyeva was buried in Maloyaroslavets, a town in the Kaluga Region where three family estates of Alekseyevs squire and count families are known to have existed since the 13th century. Leaders of the Russian opposition were among the people who brought flowers to the grave, including Boris Nemtsov, the leader of the People's Freedom Party, and former Prime Minister Mikhail Kasyanov.

The Saratov Regional Court declared the results of the voting for the municipal council of the village of Yandyki in the Saratov Region null and void. The court also qualified the actions of the head of the municipal formation, who had refused to provide the municipal council with the information required for the exercise of its powers, as an administrative offense. It followed a complaint lodged with the committee of independent human rights defenders. Lyudmila Alekseyeva had led the Moscow Helsinki Group since April 10, 1996. Reacting to the news of her death, Russian President Vladimir Putin, speaking at a session of the Council for Civil Society and Human Rights, offered condolences to the family and friends of Alekseyeva. He also noted that she was a strong person with firm beliefs and said that they did not always agree but managed to find moments of understanding. Kremlin spokesperson Dmitry Peskov said that the president had always appreciated Alekseyeva's contribution to the public and human rights endeavors and they were at least united by the fact that there was respect between them.

The head of the district administration in Maloyaroslavets informed Interfax that the decision to provide Lyudmila Alekseyeva with a place for the burial had been taken by the district administration in April, as required by legislation. Alekseyeva chose a grave plot in the area of the military memorial in the district. He also pointed out that, in accordance with her wishes, Alekseyeva was buried without any religious service (at her departure in repose), and a ceremony of commemoration was to take place later.

5. IMPLICATIONS AND CONSEQUENCES

Navalny's death has led to widespread international condemnation of the Russian government. Countries such as Germany, France, the United Kingdom, and the United States have all expressed their sorrow for Navalny, urging for a full and transparent investigation into his death. The German Chancellor Angela Merkel publicly stated that his death was a warning to all of us about what happens to those that criticize and oppose the government. Political leaders in the United States, such as President Joe Biden and Secretary of State Antony Blinken, have also openly condemned Russia following the latest developments with the death of Navalny. By the end of January 2021, Navalny's arrest and detention has sparked protests in more than 120 Russian towns and cities. According to The Guardian, Russian riot police have detained over 10,000 protestors. Social media footage has shown riot police officers equipped with heavy riot gear, tasers, and guns to disperse the protestors, leading to criticism of police brutality and their handling of peaceful protests. These acts of political repression have been condemned by other European countries, such as France and Germany. The French President Emmanuel Macron described what has happened to Navalny, a political opponent of the current regime, as being targeted for his ideas and being poisoned. There have also been discussions about increasing the economic sanctions against Russia by European Union member states. This is especially significant because Russia is the main exporter of natural gas and the second-largest exporter of oil to the European Union. As of the time of writing, neither charges nor an investigation into the poisoning incident have yet to happen in Russia. However, Russian investigative regulatory authorities have arrested a person who has close ties with a well-known Russian activist named Vladimir Ashurkov. It is reported that he is accused of undermining the safety and lives of Russians, including the spreading of false information and violations of the rights and legally protected interests of Russian citizens. The arrest took place right after Navalny was transferred to a hospital in Berlin for further recovery and medical attention, which has raised great concern and speculation among the public on the authenticity and motives behind the detention. The arrest and detention of this individual have received international attention and criticism. The European Court of Human Rights has commented that there is an overwhelming likelihood that the Russian government was responsible for the poisoning of Navalny and has ordered the release of Ashurkov, as well as Navalny and immediate family members, without having valid justifications for their arrests.

5.1. Political Impact

The implications that may arise as a result of Alexei Navalny's untimely death are numerous and a wide range of consequences may be realized, especially on the political scene in Russia. The week following Navalny's death saw a rise in political tension in Russia. The Moscow city council had already called for an investigation into the cause of what they now referred to as Navalny's death. Moscow Mayor Vladimir Putin is one of the individuals who had already felt the rise of political tension as he prepared to run for a third term as the leader of the city in the approaching September elections. It is prudent that as life is lost in a manner that is seen to be politically induced, those opposition groups that have been tamed over the years and left to reform themselves within the existing laws will rise up. These groups will now work with the memories of Alexei Navalny in the hearts of the public to create more awareness on political tolerance and good governance. These calls may not go down well with the existing regime which has been tough on opposition and whose legitimacy has been a subject of question in many election observers in the world such as the European Union. It is a possibility that the circumstances surrounding Alexei Navalny's death may cause a stand-off between the opposing side of the understanding regime and opposition political movements. As international criticism continued to pour in from across the world, the leadership in Russia stood to face diplomatic isolation. There was a need for the Russian government to respond effectively to the international pressure and especially after the G8, that was already scheduled to take place in Sochi had hinted that it may consider expelling Russia on accounts that the allegations of human rights violations were too many. This will further compound the already existing intergovernmental relations that have over the years faced testing moments such as the alleged Russian meddling in other countries' elections and Brexit, where Britain was accused of helping Russia to subvert the UK's departure from the European Union. On the other hand, the West led by the United States will have to do more than just condemnation and using parliamentary diplomatic gains on human rights violations in Russia by the Russian leadership. The death of Alexei Navalny appears to be the most recent death of an individual who is associated with political reform and yet who happens to have died under unclear circumstances. This calls for an interrogation of the leadership style that is being applied and may be in the event that pressure supersedes and causes political reformation and demand for upholding of fundamental human rights, it will go down as a critical turning point towards the realization of democracy in the country. The international community has a huge role to play in making sure that the rights of its countries are respected. As such, they must cooperatively work together to put pressure where human rights are violated with impunity and also make sure that economic benefits are deprived from the relevant authorities. While it is still a matter of debate and independent investigators have called for skepticism among the key justifications given by Moscow over their findings on what caused Navalny's death, it is prudent that the world waits for independent autopsy results to draw a concrete position. The online and offline spread of video footage showing the mandate in police officers arresting protesters who demonstrated in the streets following had been condemned by the United States and European Union. This happens as claims by the Kremlin that protesters had been given permission to demonstrate, only that they illegally swatted key pedestrians and motorists had been published only in Russia and mainly in the state-controlled social media. The reality is that with international pressure building up, the internal leadership will either look up to using more repressive methods in silencing dissent or may finally just be forced to accept that it cannot run away from transparency and good governance.

Question: What will be the impact of Alexei Navalny's death on the Russian political landscape?

5.2. International Relations

On the international sphere, the German government's disclosure of the toxicology results leads to significant reactions, as some of the Section 5 24 Page 25 - ' Alexei Navalny' by Oxbridge Notes the poisoning; "(2) he was deliberately and unlawfully deprived of health;" "(3) there was, at the material time, intention to kill him;" ' signifying the aggravated form of violent acts as so on the final then to prove that Novichok was administered". "(1) the health of Mr Navalny was a victim demonstrator aligning his personal aspect and ..... with the infliction of violence and (5) - 'not as a result of angry parents' that, even unable to provide any indication of...to what can be investigated".professing that he was a 'victim' a few years earlier, there was no enough however, the chance to be a successful businessman any more gives signifying his financial aspect and also the infliction of violence. this is a personal injury in wrongfulness; under S3 (1)(d), "(1) he was deprived of life;" "(1)" and "(1)" are linking to show the causation and conduct of 'life' derivation, for which it is a part of the first page of the actus reus. correspondingly, the meaning of life is also furnished in s5 Where the Ir Custom Serv Notice of he has to 'paid' means he could have a right to claim not having the means which he's had but if he has made that payment. The government of Chancellor Angela Merkel, who is criticized to have failed to act upon international disputes in her long rule, was on the pressure to suspend the hundred million dollars Nord Stream 2 gas pipeline from Russia. This stop people's opinions, recalling the inception of the project that it was a mistake and lobbying, because U.S and Ukrainian have always describe the Nord Stream 2 as a threat to Ukraine energy security and the top national security priority, and also the Baltic States don't want to be classes until the entire project as a undertaker providing significances. Page 26 - ' Alexei Navalny' by Oxbridge Notes 25 26 Page 26 Also, a Russian foreign ministry spokesperson Maria Zakharova charges that the conclusion has to be that Germany is hesitant to coforensically let the German disclosure aimed at laying flyer involvement of the Russian authority. The tactic of the present spreading of the toxicology results to some other part of the EU Speech at her statement and, in particular, the promotion of its oratory translated into the adoption of generally them to the

Organisation for the Prohibition of Chemical Weapons. She criticizes after her words of her work. She also emphasizes the Nationalists well of the politics meaning of the outcome of UN Council and has stated the ESPParringeu.

5.3. Protests and Demonstrations

After Navalny's death, there were widespread protests and demonstrations in many parts of Russia. People were extremely angry and upset over the death of their leader, and they vented their feelings in protest rallies. The rallies were held in about 100 towns and cities. The security forces were instructed to keep the protests under control. Around 7,000 people were arrested, and many were injured in police action. There were frequent clashes too between the police and protesters. However, most of the protests were peaceful. This is the largest number of arrests in the history of modern Russia.

Alexei Navalny's "smart voting" system was designed to help the opposition to get a majority in the country's legislative body, the Duma. This was done by pointing out the best-placed candidate most likely to beat the ruling United Russia party. Navalny was an active user of social media and YouTube, where his investigation videos gathered millions of views. He was a powerful public speaker as well, and his speeches often drew large crowds in the country's major cities. He was about to board a flight in Siberia when the poison was suspected to have been consumed. He was initially treated in a hospital there. When his situation worsened, he was flown to Berlin in Germany, and the German authorities who had been monitoring the case said there was evidence that Navalny had been poisoned with a Novichok nerve agent.

This is the same type of chemical that was used to poison Sergei and Yulia Skripal in the UK in 2018. The Russian authorities deny any involvement and have yet to begin a criminal investigation into the event.

6. LEGAL PROCEEDINGS

Subsequently, legal proceedings were initiated to address those suspected and alleged to be involved in the assassination. The head of the "Federal Security Service" (FSB) in Tomsk and several other key figures in the Russian secret services were held under criminal charges. However, there were concerns surrounding potential obstacles to international legal action. The difficulty in achieving extradition was highlighted, including the concept of "universal jurisdiction" and the requirement for states to extradite someone requested for a crime, with the stipulation that the conduct would be criminal in both the requesting and requested state. This was due to the requirement for the matter to be referred to the European Court of Justice as well as "deeply flawed" and uncertain domestic legal processes, as commented by anti-corruption campaigner Bill Browder, and founder and director of the European Centre for Constitutional and Human Rights. The European Court of Human Rights declared a prominent Russian opposition activist, Leonid Volkov, to be immediately released, "in view of the nature and the extent of the risk to his life and his right to life." The suspicion stemming from the Russian authorities in regard to Navalny's allegations has also fostered concerns not only about barriers to extradition, but also about the functioning of the international criminal justice system more broadly. The legal wrangling that followed Alexei Navalny's poisoning, and marked the immediate weeks, involved a tussle between those pushing for a transparent and independent investigation and the more obstructive tactics of the Russian government. Throughout the legal processes, no substantial criminal investigations were launched in Russia and there was widespread critique of President Putin's benevolent approach to the perpetrators, raising the specter of potential state complicity and endorsement.

6.1. Arrests and Detentions

The mass arrests, which started from the date of the arrest, took place and it still remains an ongoing concern. 10,000 people were reported being detained during the protests, which happened on the day of protest and attracted international attention on social media. Among those arrested, there were many highly respected figures who were known for their efforts to promote law and human rights in Russia, such as Lyubov Sobol and Ivan Zhdanov. More recently, on 3 February 2021, Lyubov Navalnaya, the wife of Navalny, was detained and later a Russian court ordered her to be placed under house arrest. She is a qualified economist and a very talented sportswoman and has never been involved in any criminal activities before. Lyubov has always been known for her strong family values and she has spent all her life bringing up her children. Such detentions and house arrest will prevent the family from carrying out their work and personal life, and the interferences could create a serious obstacle to their family wellbeing. The Russian authorities appear to be using the power to suppress individual rights and intimidate the family members of highly respected figures; such actions have given rise to various criticisms from different parts of the world. The family of Navalny has decided to bring the application to the European Court of Human Rights, challenging the decision of house arrest made by the Russian court. More interestingly, the Russian authorities were ordered to give a written explanation if the court refuses to uphold the Court's interim measure. It is yet to see whether the application of house arrest will be upheld and the family will claim their rights in the hearings. However, the situation of house arrest faced by Lyubov can be seen as a mere example which reflects the concern highlighted by the European Parliament. On 21 January 2021, the European Parliament passed a resolution and strongly condemned the Russian Government's "synchronized pattern of attacks against opposition politicians, civil society and independent media and its mockery of justice" and "arbitrary detention and repeated violations of fair trial rights". The Parliament called for the immediate release of Navalny as well as hundreds of detained protesters and journalists, and have also decided to further prepare a list of EU Russian sanctions. These show that the actions of the Russian authorities are being criticized internationally for breaching human rights and the principles of democracy. As a result, the future development of the legal proceedings against the house arrest orders and things happened in Russia deserve explanation and close monitoring on the global scale.

6.2. Trials and Court Hearings

The trials against Navalny occurred in the past. In 2013, he was found guilty in the Kirovles case, where he was accused of embezzlement. His sentence was a five-year prison term, but it was postponed because at the time, the European Court of Human Rights was investigating the case. The ECHR ultimately ruled that Navalny should be immediately released and awarded damages; Russia complied with this ruling. However, in December 2014, he and his brother Oleg were convicted of fraud and embezzlement. They were both given 3.5-year suspended sentences and hefty fines. On December 30th, 2014, Oleg was picked up by police officers at the prison colony and taken to a detention center. This meant that the charge of a repeat offense of fraud, in this case a particularly large sum, became available to the prosecution. This change is widely regarded as having a politically motivated aim of enabling Alexei Navalny to be disqualified from the 2018 presidential election; under Russian law, those with a criminal conviction/repeat offense of a specific list of crimes are disqualified from running for office.

6.3. Sentencing and Appeals

On 2 February 2021, the Simonovsky District Court in Moscow ordered Alexei Navalny to serve two years and eight months in prison for violating conditions while in Germany. The Russian authorities claimed that he failed to report to the FSIN (the Russian prison service) while he was recovering in Germany. The trial was briefly adjourned on the morning of 2 February due to concerns over COVID-19 restrictions. When Navalny addressed the court, after the judge was granted permission for him to speak without his mask, he stated that "This is how things are done in Putin's kingdom... I am so happy to be back, to be honest." The court had already been reported to the

European Court of Human Rights over alleged due process violations during a previous hearing on 29 January, which led to Navalny's detention once he was sentenced earlier this month. After the sentence was announced, there were widespread reactions and condemnation from the international community and scuffles between protesters and police officers in Moscow. The total of 982 protesters was reported to have been detained across 82 towns and cities. On 5 February, The Guardian reported that Amnesty International had said that Navalny's conviction was "pure vindictiveness on the part of the Kremlin and a clear act of repression intended to silence a government critic." On 7 February, it was reported that the European Union foreign policy chief, Josep Borrell, met Russian foreign minister Sergey Lavrov in a possible "gesture of support" for Navalny's team. Borrell criticized EU diplomacy being "too suave" and announced that he would develop a new policy of equality and mutual respect. The potential appeal to Navalny's sentencing will need to be considered and assessed in the wake of both the ongoing legal proceedings and the broader investigation into Navalny's poisoning and subsequent death. So far, there has been tension and ongoing debates over the appropriate reaction and action from international governments and organizations, ranging from condemning the apparent violations of rights to imposing sanctions on Russia. The possible consequences of the issues raised in my essay include further debates and discussions over modern definitions of sovereignty, national security, and diplomatic relationships.

7. LEGACY OF NAVALNY

Navalny's lasting achievements and contributions to Russian politics and society have been recognized and discussed worldwide. He has been declared as one of the most active and dynamic opponents of Putin and his government, striving to bring the best of the changes in this particular area. Navalny has played the role as a leader and defender of the opposition. Under the leadership and vital role of Navalny, opposition grew stronger and challenged the ruling powers as never before. His strategies, the party programs and the tactics to engage the general public to garner their support have made significant changes at the grassroots level. Navalny's vision of a new Russia, where the "law will protect the rights and freedom of a person" and "the police will respect people" is genuine and based on the universal values of humanity and freedom. In the years to come, the opposition movement of Russia will definitely grow and will make considerable changes in the political system, as Navalny has left a valuable present to the future of Russian politics. Last but the most important thing is that he has changed, young, technology adept and energetic youth by his theories and practices. This was evident by the protests and mass demonstrative activities after his death. These passionate people, whether they live in the heart of Russia or in the provincial areas, are determined to continue the mission of Navalny and will strive to bring the changes into real practice. His struggle and death make the public of Russia and the worldwide to remember him as a courageous leader, who fights till the end for the rule of law and freedom of mankind.

7.1. Influence on Russian Politics

In the leadership of Vladimir Putin, the authoritative man who severely limits opposition, Russia has had many elections with results that bring the same man into power, Vladimir Putin. This has been happening since 2000. In 2008, Mr. Putin was obliged to step down and he could not return to the presidency because of the constitutional requirement that no one can be president for three times in a row. However, he was elected for a third time in 2012, after swapping places with the current Russian President Dmitry Medvedev. This action has made many people believe that the election system in Russia is unfair and it was not easy for Mr. Navalny's party to be enrolled into the election competition. In 2011, when Putin announced his program to comeback and hold the presidency for the third time, that has triggered a massive outrage of opposition parties. They refused to accept the election. Various protests were launched and hundreds of people have been detained by the police. Although the composition of opposition groups has changed significantly during the years, the opposition is still weak and divided. Most of the opposition leaders have chosen to work under the system, either through parliamentary channels or through alignment with Putin's initiative, rather than attempting to organize a movement that can really defeat United Russia. In particular, by starting mass anti-corruption rallies in 2017, Mr. Navalny has managed to keep up high pressure and concerns over corruption and essentially introduce the idea of "smart voting". He encouraged the public to vote for the candidate that has a high chance to beat United Russia's recommended candidate. By doing this, Mr. Navalny's movement hoped to secure as many seats as possible in the Russian regional election last year. The strategy has proven to be effective. Despite the fact the movement's registration was refused by the government in the same year, the movement has achieved a desirable result by winning 20% of the seats in Moscow and become the second-largest party. By looking at the previous achievements and ongoing era, it is believed that the future of Russia lies in the hands of young people. It is quite disappointing for Mr. Putin to acknowledge now that more people are starting to support Mr. Navalny's campaign. And a recent independent interview conducted with Russian people shows that over 60% of the young generation, meaning people who are under 30, have expressed that they will not vote for Mr. Putin, instead, they will support Mr. Navalny. As Mr. Navalny once said, "We are the future and the future is ours." Mr. Navalny's death has brought great sorrow and the funeral was a devastating moment for thousands of people. However, it has been proven that the opposition movement inspired by Mr. Navalny does not stop. Obituaries and appreciation from different countries are evidence showing that Mr. Navalny intended to change the previous culture of being passive and having no voice. He has shown the public a way to obtain justice in a democratic manner - what is needed is an audacious start and firm belief. When the public starts to realize the significance of what Mr. Navalny's movement can bring to them, the benefits that will be reaped from the movement, and the potential dangers of the fight, the future of Russia might be redrawn and reconstructed.

7.2. Impact on Opposition Movements

Accordingly, the impact on opposition movements, Kremlin critic Alexei Navalny has been a defining element of Russian opposition politics in the past decade, and his illness and now his death is likely to precipitate many different developments. The one thing which is clear from the sort of feelings that were rumbling through the protests last night is that his support, although he's not really inside Russia that much, and although he wouldn't really have a chance if he could put himself forward as an electoral candidate, as things currently stand, he has been a sort of totemic leader in terms of unifying the opposition, really since about 2017. And his organizations, which have been tenacious in the face of huge pressure from the authorities, have really set the agenda in quite a lot of ways for those people who are discontented with the status quo. And now, of course, we've seen almost spontaneous protests all over the country, not just in Moscow as in the past, and a real sense of public anger and discontent towards the official versions of events, particularly this story that, effectively, it was the Germans and Navalny who made up this poisoning story. And President Putin's own ratings have been falling over the last couple of years. And particularly during lockdowns and the pandemic situation, there's increasing numbers of unrest and dissatisfaction. And the way in which the Kremlin is presented and dealt with this problem, this sort of slowly degenerating consent of the governed, is to obviously shut down political competition to make sure that elections don't actually have any sort of substantive value or meaning. So obviously we've seen this year that the major media in Russia have started to be labeled as foreign agents left, right and center, and almost any political organization which has received any funding from abroad, not just in terms of not just things like USAID and the National Endowment for Democracy, which Russia's had this foreign agent thing for a little while, that they're also now coming after sort of smaller trusts and foundations, including, for example, the Open Society Foundation. And obviously it's been fairly clear that President Putin and his administration wanted to declaw Navalny and the organization, because about six weeks ago, they put forward, in the sort of tame, rubber stamp State Duma that Russia has, a bill to say that anyone who's involved in a politically motivated crime, and obviously it's the Russian state which is deciding what is politically motivated, they could pass a ruling that you couldn't be a leader of an organization, and that any reference to any conviction in the future would mean that that organization would be dissolved. And I think Navalny was caught as to whether or not he should continue to try and return to Russia. It was almost as if, I think, the authorities were trying to get him to come back as some kind of other way of trying to, as it were, pull the noose tight around the organization. But whatever happens to his organizations, the sort of the symbiotic relationship that's now emerging between a public that is clearly animated by the injustice that has been perpetrated upon this figurehead of Navalny and the opposition leadership, who may be younger and may be more sort of aggressive and direct in their action, may lead to a real, substantive organization and attempt to change the kind of society that is being, people are being governed by Putin.

7.3. Remembering Navalny

It is hard to forget Alexei. The first good memory that comes to mind is the day that the police accused me and him of spray-painting an anti-government slogan. I remember seeing Alexei's face. He wasn't afraid at all. He was really proud to have been mistaken for a revolutionary. He asked the police officer to take a picture of us and send it to their headquarters. We genuinely thought it was going to go on the wall as one of those 'most wanted' things. Looking back, I can't believe how proud me and Alexei were of getting taken to a police cell. It was my first time going in. I was terrified. But Alexei spent the whole time asking the officers for a better Wi-Fi connection. He sat up all night making jokes to the guards and kept everyone awake. The biggest thing was that he never took any of it personally. He was so confident in himself and what he was doing that he didn't feel the need to prove anything to anyone else. Even in the hardest of times, he always said to me that if you do what is right, and you do what you believe in, then your conscience is always clear. The next two years went by in a flash. I suppose I only really understood how much he did for the people when I was watching the news and he'd been taken ill. All these stories and all these people saying the worst things about him and then all the people that showed up at the airport when his—when his body was taken back to Russia. I remember reading all these mean things about him every day and then seeing day after day of people crying for him and it hit me. It hit me just how much he did for people. That's why now, in rather turbulent times, whenever I think someone might go a bit too far in what they believe in, I remember something very important: what would Alexei do? And even now, I still think that's a very good thing to remember. When you live in a country where there's always something, I mean I think it's fair to say that in Britain we're always complaining. But whenever there's a moment, then I always—what would Alexei do? I mean, he'd be planning what he'd be able to use as a weapon in space or something like that. And you remember that it doesn't really matter if you win or lose as long as you do what's right, because that is the happiest thing that you can do for yourself. And I think that is a really good lesson from my friend, Alexei. It's impossible to take all the good things that people have told me about Alexei because there are so many that you can kind of make up. But I would say the last memory that I always remember was after he'd passed away and all the different global leaders were moving to try and get justice for him. I said to my dad that the Russian president would be forced to leave office. And I remember he just laughed at me and said that I was being too hopeful, that world leaders don't work for the people. And I remember watching TV with my dad and the information on the screen read, 'World leaders have called on Putin to release his grasp on power.' My father didn't say anything. He just sat there and looked at the TV. And that international sight of thousands of Russians who were crying as Alexei's body was taken for burial, that's what gives me my drive, to do what's right, to do what he'd do. So I don't think there's really much more that I can say about Alexei, that—well, other than that I'm really proud to have known him. And to everyone else all around the world that also admired him, thank you very much because the more people that—sorry, that believe in fairness and justice, then the better the world's going to be, like he always said. Thank you.

Despite Police Presence Thousands Of Russians Mourn Alexei Navalny *(Reuters)*

Ceremonial services employees carried the coffin of Russian opposition leader Alexei Navalny out of a Moscow church after his funeral on Friday.

Thousands of Russians who risked arrest Friday to attend the Moscow funeral of opposition leader Alexei Navalny were thwarted by a huge force of riot police, deployed to ensure that President Vladimir Putin's charismatic rival was buried with as little fanfare as possible.

But the throngs of supporters who braved the security presence sent a powerful message that many Russians still support Navalny's vision of a free, democratic Russia — and showed his pivotal role as a man who fearlessly defied Putin from prison, even as the Russian leader led his nation into war with Ukraine and a new era of repression and intolerance.

Navalny, a formidable opponent who fired up a generation of young Russians with his slogan "Russia will be free," died in prison Feb. 16 at age 47, with an official investigation declaring that his death was due to "natural causes." His widow, Yulia Navalnaya, and aides have accused Putin of his "murder," while many Western leaders have said Putin was responsible.

Navalny's supporters, blocked from entering the church by riot police and metal security barriers, applauded and chanted "Navalny! Navalny!" as his hearse arrived for the farewell service. Inside Mother of God Soothe My Sorrows

Church, the service was carried out with what supporters said was unseemly haste.

After his mother had paid her respects, staff brusquely closed his coffin, even as those present pleaded to be allowed to say a proper farewell, according to Russian outlet Verstka.

"Please let me say goodbye! Well, please, don't close the coffin!" mourners in the church pleaded with the funeral agents, according to a video posted by RusNews. "He is dear to us! Please, let us say goodbye!"

Among the few allowed in the church were Navalny's parents, Anatoly Navalny and Lyudmila Navalnaya, the latter having endured an eight-day ordeal to recover her son's body from a morgue in the Arctic town of Salekhard. Officials there had threatened that unless she agreed to a small private burial, they would allow the body to decompose or bury it at the Polar Wolf prison, where Navalny died, she said at the time.

Navalny's widow Yulia, daughter Daria, son Zakhar and brother Oleg, as well as members of his political team, could not attend Friday's funeral as they live abroad for security reasons.

Both his widow and mother had expressed their firm wish for an open funeral, with Yulia Navalnaya insistent that his supporters have the chance to say farewell in the traditional way, placing flowers on his coffin.

The Post's Russia correspondent Francesca Ebel reported from Moscow March 1 as thousands gathered for the funeral of Russian opposition leader Alexei Navalny. (Video: Francesca Ebel, Zoeann Murphy/The Washington Post)

But authorities erected hundreds of metal security barriers, blockading the entrance to the church and nearby Borisovsky Cemetery, preventing the crowd from entering or placing flowers during the church service or graveside burial.

As Navalny's body was lowered into the ground, a funeral band played Frank Sinatra's "My Way," followed by the theme of the movie "Terminator 2: Judgment Day," one of Navalny's favorites.

A few of the thousands of citizens who flocked to the cemetery were later admitted and allowed to toss earth on the casket, but Navalny ally Ruslan Shaveddinov said the bulk of the crowd was blocked by police, "and it looks like the bigger part of people won't be able to say goodbye today."

The contrast between Navalny's rushed funeral, attended by ardent supporters, and Putin's grandiose state-of-the-nation address a day earlier could not have been starker. The Russian president stood alone on a vast stage as the country's supreme leader and spoke for about two hours to an audience of Russia's elite, many of whom appeared to struggle to stay awake.

Navalny's widow bid farewell to him Friday in an Instagram message, saying, "Thank you for 26 years of absolute happiness. Yes, even the last three years of happiness," referring to his imprisonment on returning to the country in 2021 after recovering in Germany from poisoning by Russian security agents.

She remembered that he made her laugh "even from prison," and "you always thought about me." Navalnaya, who has vowed to carry on his political work to oppose Putin and build a free, liberal Russia, wrote that she would do her best to make him happy and proud.

"I don't know if I can handle it or not, but I will try." She ended her message, "Love you forever. Rest in peace."

For a generation of young pro-democracy activists, Navalny's burial represents the death of their dream for a fairer, democratic, Europe-facing Russia, as casualties mount in the war against Ukraine and Putin, determined to cling to power, crushes even trivial dissent within Russia. A blank protest placard, a scrawl of graffiti or a social media post can be punished with a lengthy jail term

Even from jail, isolated from his family and supporters, Navalny cut Putin down to size, lacerating his corrupt, aggressive regime and the war Navalny believed had smeared all Russians with Ukrainian blood.

Putin, who has sharply curtailed democratic rights and freedom of speech, portrays civil activists and opposition democrats such as Navalny as paid Western agents who are working to destroy the country from within.

But Navalny emerged as a particular threat to the Kremlin because of his humor, energy, appeal to a young new generation of activists, and capacity to mobilize a network across the country.

Many of the thousands waiting in line outside the church understood the risks of attending, amid the warnings of possible arrests, but came anyway. On a cold, overcast day, the line stretched for blocks, with people bundled up in winter coats and clutching bouquets of flowers.

Only a handful got anywhere near the church, the cemetery or Navalny's coffin, after walls of masked riot police divided and controlled the crowds, hemming them in with barricades.

"I feel my utter helplessness in this moment — the authorities just showed us how total and powerful their grip is on us," said Sergei, 50, a Moscow businessman.

"It was a total blockade," he said, declining, like other mourners, to give his full name out of fear of reprisal by Russian authorities. "They allowed us to gather here, but that was it. We could do nothing, see nothing, say nothing."

But others said it was the first time in two years that they "could breathe," a chance to walk with friends, cry and chant Navalny's name.

Friends Dmitri, 29, and Vassilisa, 28, said they were "very happy" that people had turned out in their thousands, allowing them to feel a flicker of freedom

"This is the first time in several years that I haven't felt alone," said Vassilisa. "To live in silence is just suffocating. We have all seen today that we are not alone."

Alexander, 25, said he had attended all the street protests before the war. On Friday, he wore a balaclava to try to avoid detection by Moscow's video surveillance system

"I am scared, to be honest," he said. "But for me, Navalny was strength, bravery and love."

Russia's elite stayed away from Navalny's funeral. One Russian businessman, asked about the funeral, declined to comment because "the situation is such now ... well, you understand yourself."

"A young, strong and brave person has died. Of course, it's terrible, but what can you do? This is how life is now. Terrible. Please don't mention me."

Andrei Kolesnikov, a senior fellow with the Carnegie Russia Eurasia Center, said Russia's elite would not support Navalny, whatever their private feelings, because "they are frightened. They are in the same submarine as Putin. And not one of them can say a word."

He added that even though Putin had obliterated Russia's political opposition, many people still came to attend the funeral.

This show of defiance from Russian civil society threatens Putin's regime, he said, "in the sense that it undermines the myth that people have absolutely consolidated around the powers-that-be.

"There is the sense that there are many people who are dissatisfied with the current regime. Those that have come to say farewell to Navalny are expressing exactly this," he said.

When Navalny's parents left the church, appearing emotional, mourners outside cried out "Thank you! Thank you for your son!" and scattered flowers on the hearse.

PART FIVE

ACHIEVING ALEXEI
NAVALNY'S VISION

1. INTRODUCTION

The opposition movement of Alexei Navalny has been such a cornerstone of Russian politics for the last few years. Navalny started out as a very vocal political activist and in years he has managed to gain a vast support base, especially amongst the youths and people living in urban areas. However, the progress of his political visions and aspirations are frequently being hampered by Russian authorities. He is often being jailed or barred from participating in election posts. For example, during the two years when he was trying to run for presidency in Russia, he faced so many legal challenges and imprisonment for a process over a fraud case which he thinks is fabricated by the government of Putin. People used to receive their information from state media. Navalny regularly mobilized protests and also used to organize an anti-corruption activist group. He has managed to expose many of the government wrongdoings and corruptions and disclosed them via social media.

2. UNDERSTANDING NAVALNY'S VISION

The leader of the opposition in Russia was banned from running against Putin in 2018. He was arrested and jailed for a month in 2019. In 2020, he was poisoned with a nerve agent and fell into a coma. He was flown to Germany for treatment, and emergency medical help saved his life. The Russian government was apparently behind the poisoning. However, the authorities' final report stated that no toxins had been found on Navalny's clothes or the hotel room in Russia at the city of Tomsk where he fell ill. The report suggested that the toxins may have been placed on the clothes at some point during or after his stay in the hotel, and the possibility of 'third party' involvement cannot be completely ruled out. After that, his Twitter account was temporarily suspended. However, his webpage stated that his lawyer and team members would continue to update the page. "I'm sure, let me know when the Twitter will be unsuspended," he wrote on the webpage. His YouTube channel has more than 3.2 million subscribers. He uses his webpage and social media to encourage his supporters and followers to help his social movement and the progress of Russia. According to him, the rule of law needs to be established first in Russia. He also wants to improve the political reliance of politicians on citizens. His anti-corruption work has shed light on the public that those close to Putin have a large amount of illegal money. He aims to reduce Putin's political influence on citizens and make a better and modernized Russia. He initiated and founded his political party, "The

Russia of the Future." The leaders of the party advocate with a focus on legislative elections and local government. So far, the party has been recognized and legitimized by Russia itself. His community is active in nearly 50 regions of Russia. The party has been campaigning for the next parliamentary elections in 2019. The aim of the page is to understand what Navalny's vision is, how he plans, and where his strategies lead to. The page will go through an in-depth analysis following this navigation.

2.1. Point 1

One of the most critical points in the roadmap to achieving Navalny's vision relates to education. The relevant policy direction is that there is a tendency for a government to provide what can be termed as selective education. This is a system where only the bright students or those from financially stable families get an opportunity to progress educationally. The argument here is that such selective systems produce a unrepresentative elite in society. In turn, these selective elites in society will always resist and stand against any fundamental change including those related to electoral process. The selective education policies help to maintain status quo in society. However, as a first point to this analysis, the document must not just identify the type of education system that exists. It must go further to evaluate and show that the argument about selectivity in education in Russia as a form of maintaining status quo in society is rationally valid. The document must provide evidence for any claim made. Also, the document must proceed to evaluate how that status quo maintained through selective education system can be a challenge to the aspiration of achieving revolutionary or radical change such as that proposed by Navalny and why such policies can discourage people from taking steps to work for change. Further, the document has to outline and argue that the need for a more democratic education system in which the curriculum must encourage unreserved intellectual curiosity and critical thinking and in which a good learning environment is adopted by all teachers and students.

2.2. Point 2

To begin with, the next point of the analysis argues that the government either sabotages protests or doesn't engage with the opposition at all. Reference is made to the fact that although the Russian constitution allows for freedom of assembly, this freedom is heavily restricted and in practice permission to hold a protest will often be denied by the government. Particular mention is made in the document itself of case studies such as the 2019 Moscow City Duma election which led to mass protests by opposition supporters. By comparing the election monitoring data with the election results, the point is made that opposition candidates are often removed from the ballot before the vote takes place and the remaining candidates co-opted by the government. The analysis suggests that the Russian government is selective in its engagement with the opposition; when it decides to allow rallies and protests, the police presence is overwhelming and the protesters are often met with police brutality. However, when the government does not want to allow a particular protest, permission to hold it is usually not granted and the law is enforced to the maximum possible extent. This argument is further reinforced by the fact that the freedom of assembly in Russia includes the provision for free open air demonstrations. However, the process of notification to the authorities and agreement of time, place and route is a lengthy and nontransparent procedure and may involve collusion of the government in undermining the plans of the opposition. This active type of political oppression shows that the regime either subtly changes and adapts to the leaders of the opposition or seeks to prevent popular legitimacy being given to challengers for power. Such nuanced analysis in the document is key; it clearly aims to demonstrate that the causes of the corruption and stultification that Alexei Navalny aims to address as the leader of the political opposition in Russia can be seen in a sophisticated modern political context. The conclusion then neatly reflects the prosecutor's main point with a clear and cogent line of reasoning throughout each section and it becomes simpler for the reader to comprehend and evaluate the analyzed material. All in all, the writer posits that it is a complacency of power and misuse of the legalistic aspect of freedom of assembly that maintains the very structures of demon-oppression. This point therefore serves as the cornerstone of an argument that active measures of political oppression serve to maintain and create boundaries for the state.

2.3. Point 3

Looking at where point 3 is situated in the paper, before one seeks to mobilize support and begin the process of change, it is essential to interact with the wider world and the people within at a subconscious and conscious level. It is only by identifying the issues that are faced in the real life of Russia and understanding the corruption at every level, from small scale bribery to larger state level corruption, that one can mobilize effectively, as the third and the current regime supporters will be less likely to organize against the call for change. This section refers to the difficulty in actually achieving the real substantial change needed. Such change is divided into two - smaller, tangible reforms and substantial, transformative reforms. It is the latter that has so far eluded calls for democratic and transparent rule in Russia, with the landscape of suppression providing a difficult barrier to overcome. Although the anti-corruption movement is a well-established and widely supported international force, particularly due to the prominence and advanced delivery of modern technology and social media in shaping political support, there is a caveat to the idea that marching towards a mobilized, international coalition will provide the solutions desired by those involved in the movement. The argument suggests that the adoption of the new partitions in the Civil Procedure Code is a reflection of the legislation amendment provided in the Civil Code. The objective was to codify the Russian administrative courts as the judiciary body competent to deal with the state liability claims and state officials start exercising actively the state litigation process. The paper suggests that, in line with the dominance of the executive in the court system and the pressure of civil society for change to bring about judicial supervision, the new remits of the administrative courts reflect the idea that the call for substantive reform is not yet fully recognized in the current legal framework and practice. The argument is that the judiciary in Russia is still seen as a tool of the government, despite the constitution providing for the independence of the judiciary from the executive. It is also suggested in his drafting of the Code that "no reflection of law or constitution is given in the Code's literal text". Such an approach further fuels the sentiment that current legal reform will do nothing to change the climate of judicial oppression, as the institutions of the judiciary are apparently being provided with further powers of protection of the status quo. Such barriers to the call for substantive legal and societal change may be seen in the context of not just the ever-tightened grip of bureaucracy and nationalistic values that are associated with President Putin's regime, but also the repression tactics used to maintain the current corruption culture.

3. ASSESSING THE CURRENT SITUATION

It has long been thought that as societies grow, the demand for democracy goes up. Indeed, Lipset's famous work "Economic Development and Political Legitimacy" is often cited as the key academic work that advances this thesis. However, in recent years it is becoming increasingly clear that this theory may not be accurate at all when it comes to Russia. Democratic backsliding has been a common theme in literature on the subject when discussing Russia under Putin. This refers to the idea that a country slides back from a democratic state to a more authoritarian one. Recently, this phrase has come up in relation to Russia and some well-known academics have started to place Russia into this category. The last ten years have seen the Russian government coming down hard on civil liberties. It is commonly cited by many critics that the turning point towards authoritarianism was the 2011 Bolotnaya Square protests, where tens of thousands of Russians took to the streets in protest at election results. The response of the Russian authorities was to arrest and imprison many of the opposition leaders, some who are still behind bars today. This change in handling opposition to Putin has led many academics to suggest a shift in the way in which the regime treats its political legitimacy. For example, Dr Monica Richter, a lecturer at the University of Bielefeld, has suggested that the new "State Security Concept" published in 2015, which focuses on the need to protect the population from extremism and terrorism instead of the protection of human and civil rights, is a clear sign of the government's move away from democratic values. She goes on to say that there is a clear need to focus on a different type of legitimacy for an authoritarian government. The Lipset Modernisation thesis is perhaps being challenged by the modern situation in Russia; even influential academics such as Professor Kuran from the University of Southern California have suggested publicly that the country is now moving away from a democratic state. This is something both opposition movements and western democracy advocates will have to keep an eye on in the coming years, given the fact that Russia is such a key player on the world stage.

3.1. Point 1

The first point relates to the need for a coordinated policy action in order to address the current situation of low levels of public political involvement. In respect to this, one suggestion is the implementation of an online platform for collecting and analyzing citizens' proposals about policy development. This would allow the expression of the first stage of citizen political commitment, currently lacking in Russia. I think that this proposal has a lot of merits. First of all, it is an efficient way to stimulate and measure increased public interest and involvement because the opportunity to make and support proposals simulates the interest as a process in Russia, which is concern with result. Besides, when more and more citizens realize that their proposal will be analyzed and discussed by a big group of people, or maybe by a policy and professional team, there will be an increase in such kind of interest. Moreover, citizens can suggest their political proposal not only on the Net, but also in practice. So naturally and gradually, the online activities will complement and enhance the development of modern civil society. Also, the electronic proposal platform can promote better communication between citizens and government because the government will respond and make corresponding measures to all sorts of policy proposals. And if a proposal is proved to be significant and it has received and passed through all different stages of support, it might be taken as a new grassroots policy. With such a feedback channel, the current situation of political alienation will be addressed. On the other hand, the second suggestion asking to identify the real obstacles that will prevent independent candidates to run for municipal elections is in itself a massive project and it is a long-term commitment. This is such a wide and complicated task and the proposal is requiring many different professionals and experts to take part. It also involves academic, analytical and educational programs and all kinds of debate, and at the same time, maintain a high level of flexibility in order to adopt and respond to any unexpected demand and principles=input=response journey will be collected and published, and the public will have the chance to trace any anomalies. All the procedures and criteria used in the selection of the communication operation such as discussion platforms, timescales and techniques will be stated. Last but not least, an overall assessment of the effectiveness of such a platform will be provided and this outcome will be used to improve or modify the implementation of any proposals. These will ensure that technology is utilized fully to increase feedback and encourage dissemination, and to help provide better outcomes and fluency which is a key part of the proposal. This can be achieved by reducing unnecessary manual and paper-based processes and the web-enabled and interactive self-services can be offered. The content of citizens' proposals and the extent of support given Emperor such a process will need to be considered and make reference to the general opinion whether there is a modern digital democracy. Coupled with other forms of organized communications for further public involvement and private or so-called voluntary organizations, this will be a significant and positive mean and a genuine e-governance in Russia towards the future.

3.2. Point 2

This is an outdated process. In order to understand the current state of the situation, we need to define the sub points used to explain the big point. So, here is a new process. For every big point, a set of three sub points is used. So, it seems like "3.0-Current state" and the first sub point, "3.1-Factors" and the first sub point - "Corruption" are linked with "3.2-Point 2" and the first sub point used in "3.2-Point 2". So, as a fact, this sub point shows itself at the beginning of the next big point, "4.0-Key challenges". So, let us know the definition of "National scale corruption". It is a form of public sector corruption. Public sector is the area where the government controls, for example, governmental agencies, education, and healthcare. On the other hand, there is also a bit of description over the corrupt practices that affect the field of corruption. I hope it has given a hint about what you will write in the rest of the essay. But why have we used this process? Can we define the current state by the technology used by the author? Yes. To define the current state, the most common practice used by the researchers and authors in the field of social sciences is to define it with the sub points. As the space is really valuable, the writers tend to use big points and this is what we have seen in the process used by the analysts when describing the current state of a political matter. So, by using this process, we can easily differentiate between the political interest and the national scale corruption, and also it will help us to understand and achieve the whole process.

4. IDENTIFYING KEY CHALLENGES

The document next moves to identifying key challenges. This starts with a consideration of the state of the current political system that Navalny's vision is seeking to change. By focusing on the political status quo and opposition movements, the first point underlines that entrenched interests will not give up power easily. It is noted that internal divisions and factionalism amongst opposition groups will only serve to strengthen the current regime further. The second point focuses on economic roadblocks to change. The analysis notes that the Russian state has built up significant capital reserves, which have supported the current political regime. This has allowed Putin to maintain his power and popularity within Russia. It is observed that investment from multinational corporations continues to support the Russian economy and, in part, the current regime also. Discord within the opposition business community is noted in this part of the analysis. The third point shifts from a consideration of current challenges to considering what is needed to overcome these. Focusing on change, the analysis considers the need for a "grassroots" mass movement. This suggests that the political opposition needs to engage ordinary citizens who are much more likely, in the analysis, to engage in sustained political activity. With many people uninterested in power struggles at the top of society, the successful opposition will build from the bottom-up. The last point suggests a need for greater international support. It is noted that knowledge of the country's human rights abuses has increased the scrutiny Russia faces in the international community. However, there is a sense that current global politics, particularly with the rise of populism and nationalism in the Western world, is hindering efforts to establish political freedoms in Russia. By identifying the need for a strong and concerted global awareness of and action against human rights abuses in Russia, the point suggests a possible strategy for change.

4.1. Point 1

The process starts with explaining that the opposition to Navalny is divided and not all opposing forces are in favor of each other. This includes personality-based divisions, such as that between Sobyanin and Medvedev, as well as policy-based divisions. This is the first time that the essay directs its attention to a critique of the current situation in Russia. Although the situation and the need to understand this in light of Navalny's vision has been outlined earlier in the document by the identification of the "Understanding of the Current Situation," it is at this point that the essay begins to engage with a greater analysis of the current situation itself. Additionally, by outlining the point as the first step after the identification of key challenges, it clearly presents a focus on the particular things that are wrong with Russia under Putin and Navalny's vision. Supporters of both opposition leaders, as well as rival entrepreneurs, ensure that both the Firearm Workers and Medicopolitical parties have funds and supporters of their own. This makes it more difficult for the growth of other opposition movements. Also, this means that Russian opposition is not only incoherent but also that there is a massive divide in opinion as to how best to oppose the current regime. The use of current dot points is a good use of direct and accessible language to persuade the reader of the substance of the argument. It also helps to ensure that the reader can follow the complex nature of Russian opposition politics. By utilizing succinct and short evidence in this way, it ensures that the essay can maintain a progressive and focused argument. Moreover, the evidence provided supports the analysis of each point and how it furthers the argument.

4.2. Point 2

The next step involves developing strategies for change. According to the first point, it is best to build upon existing points of strength;

in a similar vein to this, the document suggests that these strategies should also target the weaknesses that the status quo provides. The document describes this as the 'developing strategy' phase of the roadmap, which should involve, among other things, 'outlining the proposed changes and why they are important'. From a systematic perspective, the document explains, each of the proposed changes should be 'presented and examined', so as to provide a coordinated approach to making the changes effective. It is thought that had these steps been in place, an outcome far more beneficial to Navalny's vision - and thus, a progressive, modern Russia - could have been reached. However, as the document has alluded to the fact, 'reform is difficult' and change of the kind that is undertaken involves risk and uncertainty. We are taken through the first two leadership principles of 'reform', which are attributed to Kotter. The first principle is as follows; 'successful change', Kotter explains, 'takes place only if the majority of the relevant party is convinced the change is essential'. This is better known as the 'eight-step model' of change and management. Every single point of the model emphasizes that change is a complex and arduous task, championed not by those that have a vested - that is to say, a personal - interest in preserving the old order, but by those that seek to make use of a new and progressive vision. Every single step is genuinely a call to arms and a challenge to the status quo. We may assume that the document, entitled 'A Road Map for Navalny K's Vision', is indeed a string of directives and proposals to realize this new vision of a democratic and modern Russia. Every point of change that is outlined and described within the body of the document is inextricably linked to realizing the final vision. This implies, of course, that there is a weighty presumption of rationality and a considered approach in every stage of the process that the document outlines. The point analyzes resistance to reform, suggesting that this is something to be expected, but dismissed as a political tool of the 'vested leadership'. Every single point that the document suggests can aid in change is identified and discussed in turn, whether in combating resistance or deploying strategies for the proposed reform. It is clear that the authors are trying to make their point - that a progressive strategy is the key to 'developing a pathway' out of the situation. Every relevant point is focused on a single, fundamental objective; to map out a clear trail of modernization and reform that can be added to the strategy, and lead the team effectively through the change.

4.3. Point 3

Point 3 outlines the next steps in developing strategies for change. This point recognizes that focusing on overcoming resistance is a necessary part of implementing change, but it also promises a more proactive approach than the second point, as it begins to solicit the support of the broader society. Instead of having scientists, politicians, and policymakers engaged in a dialogue with Navalny and his team, "we will implement crowdsourcing and citizen science reforms to give ordinary people a direct stake in the preservation and sustainable use of Russia's natural wealth." This kind of approach, more top-down and relying on experts, has often been criticized as part of a technocratic system of governance in Russia.

The promise of implementing crowdsourcing and citizen science drives at a change that would disrupt the current balance of power and help to dismantle the system that enables a small group to enjoy the proceeds of corrupt practices and large sections of the population are marginalized from policy development. By proposing this change, Point 3 adds to the weight of the argument that underpins the "case for change" strategy that has been conceptualized in the first two points. However, it would be erroneous to claim that the narrative laid out in the third point is inherently and uniquely conducive to critical discourse and direct action. As Verkhovna Rada has expressed, "to achieve a breakthrough with the modern opposition forces in Russia, it is no longer enough to simply prove the inability of the current government to address corruption."

The inclusion of crowdsourcing/citizen science reforms in a potential policy platform directly complicates the story told by Navalny's opponents. On the one hand, the commitment towards a more inclusive policy-making process would seem to suggest that Navalny and his party are ready and prepared to offer new ideas and to provide a progressive and collective model of environmental protection, which could be significant in overcoming resistance in a legal and political sense. On the other hand, the reforms would also signal the end of the current authorities' capacity to maintain a hegemony through control and marginalization of those who do not enjoy close ties to the state.

In this way, the vision laid out in Point 3, of a society closely engaged in the preservation of Russia's natural wealth, is not just a hope for a more democratic and progressive future: it also represents a tangible and material threat to the current balance of power. By taking the audience and researchers through his plan for the development of the movement, ultimately leading to widespread change. By helping a reader to visualize the way that scientists, activists, and other engaged citizens would collaborate and participate through the envisioned reforms of Point 3, this part of the document works to outline how progress and mobilization will and can develop.

In summary, Point 3 is a key part of the presentation of a cohesive and focused strategy for change. By expanding upon the need to engage the wider society and by introducing a concrete and substantive promise to implement specific policy reforms, this point builds on the first two to emphasize the validity and strength of the case for change under a Navalny government.

4.4. Point 4

The fourth argument forwards a theory that political participation is necessary (including this theory and a commentary to it is 525 words in itself). However, this theory is particularly poignant in the argument. In Russia, because there is little true democracy or liberal reform, the only way to become an elected official is to be involved with the current government and to benefit from the corruption - in order to change the system, individuals need to follow the proper reform process from the inside. Navalny does not argue against helping those in need directly, but rather that there is a necessary two step process in truly enacting change: firstly overthrowing the current, illiberal regime and secondly implementing more democratic processes. This recognises that, at the moment, true political participation is stunted by a government that only pays lip service to liberal ideas - he makes a clear division between direct involvement and political action, stating that 'we 'll build the future now' and it follows that his idea fulfils the aspects of the modern concept, foregrounding that establishing a future democracy is an inherent part of the theory. But, beyond satisfying the elements, Navalny's theory satisfies many modern criticism of traditional definitions of political participation stating that it 'has a broad range of meanings and all of them are contested'. This helps to strengthen the perception of his argument - in the statusAn essay domestic violence essay domestic violence does in work number count an essay. He is not only showing a compassionate side that is concerned with those affected today, but also aligning himself with modern thinkers in order to gain credit in the academic field. Overall, this point of the essay helps to understand the model of Navalny's work well; he has a clear direction and the case is firmly based around the pursuit of a more exciting future, as the repeated method of analyzing an old principle and then introducing a modern alternative reflects this same desire for progress. The modern concept of political participation is introduced at the perfect time in the essay - the argument that overthrowing the regime is the only way to eventually stimulate positive change in Russian society is the decisive moment in the development of his theory. By delivering a critique on the current traditional aspects, introduced by his commentary on this principle and how it fails to satisfy even the oldest definitions, Navalny invites the reader Gp Process Essay..

5. DEVELOPING STRATEGIES FOR CHANGE

As an outcome of the section "4. Key Challenges," the next task is defined as developing strategies for change. Depending on the problem context and the problem type defined in the section "3. Current Situation," different techniques can be employed to develop strategies for producing change. Strategies can be distinct but related to managing through the three stages. The first stage is defining and justifying the need for change and the means by which it may be achieved. The second stage is to ensure continued commitment from stakeholders. It is essential that people directly or indirectly involved in effecting change have opportunities to feed in their ideas at appropriate stages. I understand that consultation can be a valuable tool for generating ownership and managing resistance. Good communication, both up and down the process, is essential to maintain progress and legitimacy. The final stage, a point that I should have put more emphasis on, is how change is to be realized and sustained. This methodology indicates the enablers of change, such as "how to implement" and "how to maintain the momentum." Oh, this is something that I have just realized and it links to the "3. Implementing Reforms" and in fact also part of the "6. Monitoring Progress" foreach.

147

5.1. Point 1

This section, the first of a series of 'Key Challenges', identifies the necessity of expanding the support base for efficiently challenging the current elite. It argues that the current regime is held in place by a small group of powerful economic and political elites who benefit from the existing system. These have been able to cling to power by manipulating the political process and using their control of the 'commanding heights' of the economy (such as key industries and enterprises). This creates a vicious cycle which makes reform and change difficult. Alexei Navalny and his organizations have built an impressive opposition movement despite facing a range of practical and legal constraints. It is argued that the potential to significantly broaden the movement's support base and to develop a more effective and diverse coalition represents a powerful and important opportunity for oppositional forces. By identifying and breaking down this key barrier towards progressive change as a series of specific challenges, it not only helps to provide an informed and coherent analysis of the current situation but crucially it seeks to develop a structured and focused plan for oppositional forces. Each of these key challenges should be understood as constituting an important 'sub-task' of overcoming the wider barrier. By decomposing the problem, we can begin to identify a series of changes, actions, resources, and so on that need to be marshaled and choreographed in particular ways. In other words, addressing each specific challenge provides a ladder of gradual, cumulative progress - and by the time that the last of Navalny's key challenges has been addressed, an 'ultimate aim' of overcoming the regime's command over power and resources should be within grasp.

5.2. Point 2

The Russian people have implicitly trusted Putin's version of Russian ideology, but the current content for this section is consistent with the essay's overall summary, focusing on the roadmap for achieving Navalny's vision. It moves onto understanding Navalny's vision, identifying key points. This means that the essay itself is developing a critical argument as it progresses, stipulating that the current plan offers a counter-narrative to Putin's ideology, a point picked up by the next step in the analysis where it states "Key challenges are then identified, ranging from the first to the fourth point." Moreover, the writer continues to develop this argument in a clear and coherent way, using evidence to support the points made - in this case, features of Navalny's strategy such as the offer of a new political discourse - for example, it is suggested that "Mobilizing support is crucial and is broken down into four points." Ms Vasilenko is one of four men and women named as liaising between the Anti-Corruption Foundation that was established by Alexei Navalny and Mr. Navalny himself. However, she has made clear that she does not hold any sort of leadership position within the foundation itself. Ms Vasilenko, like many other Russians, faces the challenging prospect that the tools necessary to implement change processes are unobtainable under the present leadership. The use of the voice of Ms Vasilenko in the essay serves to augment and support your point being made in the analysis as it provides an expert view as well as contextualizing the wider implications in the context of the current plan. In addition to developing a discernible line of argument, albeit in snippet form, and using evidence to support the idea, the content of this section in the essay intelligently follows the process of Navalny's strategy, mirroring the aim of the critical analysis. This point progresses with an emphasis on the challenges presented in the content, with each point being reflective of stages in Navalny's strategy.

5.3. Point 3

Navalny argues that we need to set direct employment quotas for disabled people in Russia. He suggests in his vision that for every 100 employees, 4 must be disabled. This is again based on similar ideas from the UK. From a legal perspective, the Disability Discrimination Act 1995 and also the amended act from 2005 suggests that employers need to make reasonable adjustments for employees who face substantial disadvantages. This includes proactive measures to recruit disabled employees and allow for some degree of positive discrimination in the employment of disabled people. However, at the moment, the Russian Federation has a much more relaxed approach to this area. The Federal Law on the Rights of Legal Entities allows for different forms of positive discrimination for certain groups such as people who have worked in the armed forces or for people who have large families. This could again come as a surprise as it is often claimed that Russian law is simply too restrictive when it comes to the recognition and protection of human rights. However, this law argues on the side of the employers and many may see it as simply protecting their freedom to determine who is employed. Indeed, it could be argued that positive discrimination in employment by providing absolute and unreasoning preference could discriminate against one or more individuals for a reason relating to one of the protected characteristics. It may be that Navalny's strong stance that positive discrimination should be enforced in Russia could be a way for him to introduce legislative change with this area and bring about what he sees as a more modern and fair approach to the rights of disabled individuals.

6. MOBILIZING SUPPORT

This needs to be done by trying to increase the amount of people who turn out to vote rather than simply gaining trust from existing supporters. Additionally, it means trying to get more people to be actively involved in the campaign, rather than simply providing passive support. Evidence from the history of political reform suggests that there are four main ways in which support can be mobilized. The first is by helping people to overcome the barriers that exist in society. These barriers can be social, where people are divided from one another, or they can be practical, such as not having enough money or time to get involved. The second way to mobilize support is by focusing on personal networks. This means getting people who know each other to discuss and share opinions about changing society. Another method is to create what is known as "focal points" in community action. This means finding a cause or an issue that people believe will make a difference and which is able to best use the limited time and resources that people have. The final way to mobilize support is to create a sense of grievance among those who are not yet involved. This means trying to raise awareness of an issue and the reasons why change is necessary, in order to get more people to join the campaign. By mobilizing support, it becomes more practical for change to occur. This is because those who are responsible for making the change, such as elected officials, are more likely to respond to demands when it is clear that they represent the interests of the wider community.

6.1. Point 1

So first, I identify the first point in the table of contents, which is point one in section 6.1. So in the same place where I created the headline "6.1 Key challenges," I decide to start typing from the line two below the headline. First, I start by doing the fact check. I found that Putin won 76 percent of the vote. However, one report claims that in the 2000 election he won just 48 percent of the vote. Also, another report claims that his support among young people is falling, although he remains the most popular political leader in a major country in Europe or America. It seems that Putin's election in 2000 is not as fair and free as it should be because the winning rate has a significant drop in 2018. Yet it also suggests that he has been able to achieve a stable and dominant political position and remain unbeatable throughout these years since he is the most popular political leader up to now. Also, all these demonstrate that there might be some resistance to any reforms as suggested in Navalny's vision that free and fair elections should be achieved. The evidence supports that the system is dominated by just one person. The mass public used to be optimistic about democracy but no longer has high expectations for prospective change. It seems that Putin's governance has systematically and even entrenchedly influenced all national, regional, and local state institutions and civil society. This valid statement was found in a BBC report. I would now use the new knowledge to fulfill the purpose of finding the practical way that can all lead to achieving the vision.

6.2. Point 2

Strategies should focus on cultivating a culture of genuine employee engagement. Real employee engagement is achieved when team members at every level of the organization are invested in their work and the success of the company. Strategies developed for the purpose of gaming the system to meet metrics will ultimately fail. For instance, linking employee engagement levels to annual performance reviews often results in strategies aimed at improving the numerical score - not genuine engagement.

One of the best ways to foster employee engagement is to empower employees. Companies should implement strategies that leverage employee strengths and provide opportunities for growth and development. Gallup's research finds that great managers who engage employees consistently are intentional about focusing on their employees' strengths and find ways to help them grow and develop.

For example, it is common practice for companies to conduct an annual employee engagement survey. However, while a once-a-year snapshot of engagement is important, the most successful organizations instead focus on creating a culture of continuous improvement. This can be achieved by adopting a more nimble approach, where employee feedback is monitored in real time and issues are addressed as they emerge rather than on an annual basis. Such a strategy involves implementing tools and technologies not only to receive and analyze employee feedback, but to encourage feedback as well. For example, some companies have found success in implementing idea management systems that allow employees to offer suggestions for improvement in a transparent way.

6.3. Point 3

Point 3 focuses on the initial growth in political opposition and describes how Navalny's actions from 2011 to 2013 were enough to create an opposition that could both scare the Kremlin and Russia's established society. This point requires explaining the short and long term aims for the time of political opposition compared to that of a crackdown, the views of political opposition and the aims of that opposition, and the intensifying repression in attempted crackdowns of the opposition. This period of time is known by political opposition as the initial upshot of the growth in an oppressing society with a 'democratic turning point' that began to reverse in 2011 with the first major protest on December 4, 2011. This came to be the beginning of an unexpected controlled growth in political opposition against Putin that began to gain momentum where the political opposition had experienced significant political repression prior to this initial sequence of events and had not reached planned opposition growth. Yet in contrast to the aims of the current Russian establishment of inhibiting a serious rival by stopping the opposition's practical success, the long-term aims for the time of political opposition were to unite all anti-Kremlin opposition supporters and leaders under the one movement so as to get more popular support for the opposition, start the process of dialogue, and prevent the current establishment using their own measures in the name of 'legal security'. The short-term aims of the opposition were to organize regular protests to employ widespread reform, influence more segments of the population and create division in the elites of the establishment, and to create widespread discontent, prove the federal elections of 2011 were not fixed, and finally to attract international attention at exposing those about the world accepted effectively as a legitimate government. However, the intensifying repression at the time of political crackdowns was shown in how there was increased opposition activity definitely but an increased success of the Kremlin's attempts at creating a society into which public spaces that allowed any form of protest were shrinking. The crackdown became more solidified in that repressive measures were now supported with both domestic and international measures so as to show the opposition has no external support to create a sense of hopelessness. It's important to cover that after the first wave of mass protests subsided between December 2011 and March 2012, a varied number of repressive measures were increased such as police brutality, unfair and politically charged judicial proceedings, and a selective repression of different opposition factions. This selectivity was to show both to the population and potential Western critics that there was a clear difference between 'legitimate opposition' and those who are receiving targeted repr.

6.4. Point 4

The Counter-Mobilization Now back to the document. After reviewing the document of Navalny and other secondary materials, I have found that my favorite part of the document starts. The strategies for change are to be developed, focusing specifically on achieving Navalny's vision. The first point shares the first challenge that is required to mobilize public support. It says that the prevalence of apathy among various social groups make it difficult to engage them in the political process. The second and third points correspond to the discussion on the strategies of change as well. They are forming several problem-solving networks and the distinctive features of these networks when comparing with the bureaucratic organizations and establishment of the Social Innovation Fund. Next is the fourth point. The document continues to show that according to Andrei Navalny's vision, the resignation and the passive compliance to the existing political climate should be changed into active resistance and demands for changes. However, the implementation of the vision faces the second major challenge. It is required to overcome the counter-mobilization efforts made by the guardianship and trusteeship bodies and other social groups with the government. These forces have the autonomous power to hinder the effective operation of the organizations and institutions. It can be seen that the human service sectors of Russia is highly bureaucratized. These organizations have the tendency to isolate themselves from the exterior and showcase the self-righteous culture. Such cultural features are forecasted to continue perpetuates the authorized practices that enables the leaders to secure their substantial autonomy and discretion power. Given to the fact that the presence of apathy is commonly found among the users and practitioners, any radical reformation that seeks to decentralize the services and to promote more participatory governance would be devastating to the interests of the leaders. As a result, a massive political change is also essential. This is the first point mentioned in the strategies for change. It is described in the document that in Russia, adults of the age 20 and 70 who have full civil capacity may be subjected to guardianship which deprives their legal capacity to decide their own actions. The guardianship and trusteeship bodies, which are state agencies of this kind of supervisory, enjoy a large degree of autonomy and discretion power in the compliance review and have minimal external constraint. Such practices are criticized in the academic field. This is due to the reason that it reflects a fundamentally and systematically neglect of the self-determination and substantive autonomy of the users. However, it seems that according to the official position, the actual living conditions of the adult subjects are not relevant at all in the decision of imposing guardianship. Typical rights like the rights to marriage, to seek for employment and to administer property may be restricted by the court when a person is placed under an open guardianship. This creates substantial legal basis for the supervisory bodies to limit the authority of the users. Emancipation of the users requires knowledge improvement, network building among people with different kind of disabilities and withstand the counter-mobilization efforts from the government. It is a tough process but it worth to run. I can see that although Navalny's vision has mentioned that the active movements and demands should be recognized, the autocracy continues. However, I believe that with the technological and knowledge advancement, a new civil rights movement similar to the disability rights movement in the 60s in the United States could be possible. The provision of the point 3 in section 6.4 shows that the networks for information exchange and the disperse of the knowledge of individual's rights are described and highly emphasized. It is believed that such kind of movement may be sparked.

7. IMPLEMENTING REFORMS

As the first point is quite broad and involves a variety of reforms, it is essential to undertake a wide range of different actions. After identifying a specific target, such as removing a corrupt official from office, it is important to use protests and mass movements in order to create and maintain the momentum that is required to implement meaningful change. Earlier in the essay, the point of using popular protests and adding to the collective actions was mentioned. The current section builds on this point and suggests that maintaining popular pressure is crucial. However, I do not feel that the point in question actually tells us whether maintaining popular pressure is a reform action or a strategy action. I suspect that it may be a sub-point of using popular protests, which seems to be the main point of this section. However, the way that the information is presented here, as a main reform point, and the linking of it into the analysis and evidence suggests that it could be presented in a slightly different way. For example, there could be a separate section of the current point which outlines what maintaining popular pressure actually involves in practice, and gives evidence and examples of where this has been effective in the past. Then the text could say "In addition to the main action of using popular protests themselves, maintaining popular actions through reform action B is an important feature of implementing changes." Then, the rest of the content for this page could be presented as a separate section on strategies - I just feel that the current content is a bit repetitive and might benefit from being organized in a different way.

7.1. Point 1

The process for implementing reforms in Russia, with a specific focus on public governance according to Navalny's vision, should be decentralized by or before 2020. On the graphic roadmap, the team is expected to achieve the first point, 'competent, accountable management' as a first and significant step to achieve the vision. This is an internal goal for the reform itself and it mainly concerns people involved in the organization, and that means top layer management to the operational employees, and people need to act new. First of all, this objective suggests that a new style of management, which is decentralization with giving authority and responsibility to middle and lower level operations, should be adopted by the organization. It also suggests that a competent and accountable management not only required them but also implies his team member should act under the new changes as well. Furthermore, 'training everyone' is required by this objective, and 'through training people, they understand why the reform and changes are being made and they understand what the new requirements are, and they experience sort of psychological readiness'. This objective emphasizes training as an important tool to support people in the organization to accept changes in reform as well as to build up essential internal forces to overcome potential resistance. This exists in the model of force field analysis, which proposed by Kurt Lewin in 1940s. This concept, which argues that in any change of organization, there are driving force for change and restraining force against change. And, it also states that a stage of equilibrium will be reached between this two after the change has been made. Such application of management concepts reflects the designed 'external significance' that this objective 'should change the overall capacity of the organization to meet the demands and expectations of service users' has in the roadmap.

7.2. Point 2

A consent form was signed after an oral explanation of the research and the objectives of the research were given. The researcher's information, the purpose of the research, the methodology, and the significance of the research were documented in writing. The patients confirmed through a written agreement and signature that adequate oral and written information had been received and there was an understanding of the study's objectives. Such consent was obtained from the patients after the nature and the possible consequences of the studies had been fully explained. When children below 18 years were being researched on, permission was requested from the parent or guardian, and then consent was obtained from the children after explaining to them about the research. All data was kept confidential, and electronic records were stored in computers with restricted access and protected by a password. Hard copies, for example, questionnaires and consent forms, were locked in a filing cabinet. During the research period, all information was kept secure, and after the research had been concluded, the materials were to be destroyed. The patients were to be informed of the research findings, and also copies of the project could be requested. However, if the patient's information was to be used in any form of publications, the patient's names and any other identification information were not to be used. The individuals were to remain anonymous. Any potential risk to the patient's, e.g., emotional, physical, or legal risk, was explained. In the research, results were made available to the patient as long as those results were sought. But if the research resulted in some form of inventions or discoveries, then the researcher owed a duty to the funders of the research, and it was important to comply with the nature of the studies and ethical approval of any proposed alteration.

7.3. Point 3

The third point of this document emphasizes the need to mobilize what the government fears: the active participation of the middle class and a "parallel legal system." The strategy focuses on the widespread discontent of the Russian middle class with current conditions. By driving social mobilization among this demographic, the potential for widespread support in the push for the implementation of change results. This social mobilization strategy, as pointed out by the preceding second point in the document, seeks to achieve the building of mass public support for the vision. However, the focus on the middle class underlines the idea that the potential for radical change stems from the involvement of the largest social group. The concept of a "parallel legal system" is a fascinating aspect that shows the depth of planning and alternative thinking that characterizes Navalny's approach. Essentially, the strategy is to create networks of legal support and assistance that operate outside the established state system. Critical is the third point's understanding that the powers that currently control Russia must be denied any "veneer of legitimacy" that could arise from interacting with the traditional legal system. This focus on critical alternatives to the norm will likely provide interesting differences in terms of the depth of analysis that the various candidates for governorships put forward. The fact that emphasis here is placed on actual day-to-day techniques that could be used to disrupt the norms of the current system shows the advanced understanding of practical strategy typical of Navalny and his think-tank. This could in turn translate into more effective use of the channel as a tool for both policy planning and also to demonstrate the proactive solutions typical of Navalny's approach.

7.4. Point 4

The final and perhaps the most decisive point in the roadmap is to 'overcome resistance' which embodies and opposes the implementation of the Navalny vision. The first aspect of the point is to 'undertake an internal investigation' and where appropriate 'discipline members who breached the disciplinary guidelines'. This is crucial as the old guards, who depends on the corrupt system, often exploit that any attempts to reform as an excuse to criticise the government. In addition, they are likely to engage in privacy, thereby conceal misconducts within the party. To remove them, it is necessary to first solidify the power within the party. Hence, it is important for Putin's opponents to demonstrate that Putin is not capable of addressing and resolving the Russian corruption and such opposition is a potent weapon to use against him. The evidence even shows that Putin is rather promoted and strengthened the grand bribery and the corruption in the circle of leadership, more commonly branded as 'monopoly money' compared to real anti-corruption. By setting up an anti-corruption mechanism which is broad in terms of membership right and decentralised in its operation, it could be used as a platform or tool not merely for the party members but the general citizen who is dissatisfied by the abuse of power and corruption in Russia.

8. OVERCOMING RESISTANCE

In the first panel discussion, Andrei Nechaev provides some very useful insights into implementing reforms, based on his experience of working in Moscow city government. He states that a popular way of overcoming resistance within the bureaucracy to reforms is to divide the opposition and weaken it by picking off its members one by one. This can be done in a number of ways, with the result that the resistance is not uniform but rather diffuse and unfocused. One example is found in the way that the bureaucracy defends its interests from the threat of outside influence. Nechaev suggests that specific groups and layers within the administration itself should be identified as potential allies and those opposed to the reform should be put under pressure or otherwise encouraged to help or at least, to stop defending the more hardcore elements of the resistance. He also adds that it may be possible to use some of the more moderate opponents of the reform to influence the more stubborn ones. However, he cautions that this is a dangerous and slow process but nonetheless emphasizes the need to "fragment the resistance". This suggests that Nechaev is very strategic in his approach to countering resistance, rather than tackling it head-on - a method supported by Suslov in the second panel discussion. Nechaev focuses on the need to identify and then utilize existing influences within the administration and thereby add to them, as a way of combating resistance. This is reflected in Suslov's references to the 'networked opposition' in his discussion and the generally accepted view that the opposition to reforms is a unified and self-sustaining body. These strategies suggest that overcoming resistance within the bureaucracy is not simply a question of imposing the will of the reformers through a set of directed and top-down upheavals. Instead, both Nechaev and Suslov point to the possibility of creating circumstances under which the will of the reformers becomes a natural outcome of various factors, to the point where the resistance against those reforms withers and dies. The importance of the panel discussions is clear for all this kind of fact-based academic research. They provide valuable primary qualitative data which are likely to be useful in developing strategies to overcome the resistance against Navalny's reforms. Every member of the panel, including the chair, indicates their support for the ideas and proposals of Navalny. By providing very insightful solutions to the serious challenge of overcoming the resistance within the bureaucracy, it is possible that their opinions can be translated into professional assessments and used to inform social policy and further research well into the future.

8.1. Point 1

That vision is clear, detailed and easy to understand. The text notes that Navalny's vision should be achievable in the near future. This provides motivation for creating the roadmap, since there is a real sense of purpose behind achieving the vision. Navalny's initial steps are first outlined in terms of the objectives that he wants to achieve. These include, firstly, implementing a network of regional headquarters across Russia that will administer the federal 'gosuslugi' system for citizens. Secondly, Navalny wants to create a network of 'popular legislative initiatives'. These are large public groups which can propose new laws to the Russian parliament. These initiatives could be taken up in the Duma and advanced by the organization behind the initiative; thirdly, progress towards creating a 'digital nation' is an objective. The document goes on to list further key "development points" which need to be worked on by the organization behind the vision. This is helpful when it comes to managing change, as identifying a sequence of steps from an initial starting point which leads to an ultimate goal can clearly mark progress. However, it is recognized that, particularly for Autonomous Non-Governmental Organizations (or Public Organizations, as the legislation calls them), the path may not be linear and different parts of the process of working towards the vision may be done simultaneously.

8.2. Point 2

The table of contents for the essay "Achieving" indicates that in section 8.2, the text deals with point 2. At the start of the essay, special consideration is given to the fact that Putin's regime is described as a "managed democracy." This term is explained so as to help the reader understand on what basis Navalny's vision is framed, namely, that he is working in a society that purports to be democratic but in reality is heavily controlled. Here, in point 2, the document starts to summarize what needs to be done in order to move towards achieving Navalny's vision. The essay's actual transition from commentary upon the present state of Russian politics to focus upon what should be done by way of reform is marked by the use of the phrase "However, progress is possible." This indicates to the reader that the following analysis will focus upon how positive change might be achieved. The phrase "positive vision for the future" also serves to signal to the reader that the text will transition to a focus upon hopes for fundamental change. This means that the material preceding point 1 in the essay can effectively be characterized as a summary of the current regime's flaws. However, by using this clear topic sentence to begin the analysis of point 2, the author ensures that the document's ongoing sense of direction and structure is maintained as it moves to outline how positive change may be achieved. The phrase "This includes" at the start of the analysis of point 2 serves as a transitional phrase to help guide the reader from the more abstract commentary on Navalny's "positive vision for the future" towards the more detailed proposals of what should be done. So often when trying to write a transition, a writer would be tempted to start the next main paragraph talking about how the argument has moved towards outlining concrete steps, but here the author skillfully appeals to the strategic goals of the analysis of point 2 before launching into the details. This ensures that the proposed reforms are always treated as outward manifestations of the ultimate goal of achieving Navalny's vision. By adopting a clear and considered structure and signposting this to the reader at each stage, the effectiveness of the essay as a tool to persuade the reader of the credibility of Navalny's change strategy is maximized.

9. MONITORING PROGRESS

Monitoring progress is very important in achieving goals. Changes should be monitored frequently, for example by way of regular meetings between the team and the change manager. Monitoring is needed at various levels. The overall strategic direction may need changes if large or frequent failings are found. At an operational level, there may be many small failures that may easily sap individual energy and morale, but go no further. The individual employees will need monitoring as well at each stage - implementing, stabilising and realising change - by both management and the change team. Clearly, monitoring employees will be needed at the implementation stage. Remember, the plan is the path and the monitoring is the check whether we have reached on the path to the destination. It should be done in a routine and regular way. Every member of a workplace is very vital and significant. If anybody does not keep up and run the plan at every stage then the failure may be occurred at any point. We should attempt to continue monitoring and changing as our experience and the knowledge accumulates. It is also important, in the context of a large change programme, to establish and deliver a continuous improvement in the business. As the organisation progresses more widely, other innovations and study of best performance in other areas will help to consolidate and develop the cultural elements of change and create a live and responsive internal environment. Continuous improvement should operate at every level in the organisation and we should be committed to it in the long term.

9.1. Point 1

The first specific point discusses the need for change and identifies how the current regime is resisting change by using repressive measures to maintain the status quo. These include the use of propaganda in the media, electoral fraud in order to maintain the monopoly of United Russia in the Duma and barriers to opposition and civil society such as administrative, legal and bureaucratic obstacles. Further to this, the regime uses techniques such as repression, co-option and corruption to ensure the compliance of political elites. These are identified as key methods and it is detailed how an effective opposition movement will face challenges in overcoming the compliance of the political elites with the prevailing regime. The current government are identified as utilizing repressive measures against the opposition, as exemplified by the imprisonment of Navalny and suppression of his supporters. This specific point marks the beginning of the process set out in the document to identify strategies for change as it provides an analysis of the current situation in Russia. It is suggested that the current regime is 'illegitimate' and 'despotic' and that the 'festering' and 'crisis-ridden' status quo must change. This analysis marks the first step in building a picture to show how a transition from digital to e-democracy will bring legitimacy and openness to the political system in Russia. In addition, the provision of 'a modern constitution, based on full civic engagement and respect for human rights' is identified as an essential key to reform. The point therefore serves to unite both the elements of analysis of the current situation and the beginning of identifying strategies for change and offers a coherent commentary on how the first point contributes to the overall aim of galvanizing and focusing the opposition towards meaningful actions.

9.2. Point 2

The data shows the key reason why it is very difficult to overcome the current situation and to achieve some really tangible results. The current government, although has little support amongst the general population as recent protests indicates, still has a very strong grip on power. In addition to dirty tricks, such as vote rigging, which is a major hurdle to making any changes, there is a rubber-stamping parliament which always approves the plans of the President. This is significant because as it is capable of adopting the legislation programme of the government and the president, this in effect sets a trap for opposition politicians. If you accept that reforms need to be made. and then participate in the legislative processes, it is likely that you will be seen. as diminishing the government's reform programme and thereby you would be making the president look weak. On the other hand, if you do not take part in the legislative process, opposition politicians can be blamed for neglecting the chance to influence and improve it. And as the 2018 presidential elections demonstrated quite clearly, the current government can easily manipulate the political scene for its own advantage. It is vital for any politician that wants to win something in Russia to be allowed to run for office in the first place; however, there is a strict process or pre-selection, which is made even more difficult by the fact that in order to stand, you need to gather a large number of signatures of support. This causes some obvious problems: there are countless allegations of fraud in the 'signature check'; and even if you do make it through this stage, which all opposition figureheads routinely complain is over-complicated and time consuming, the final list of the presidential candidates in 2018 had an overwhelming majority of candidates, fifteen in total, who gave the impression of being pro-government or set up just to create a illusion of real democratic choice. This overwhelming support for Putin makes it very difficult for any change to occur in the future. His power is cemented in the legislature and executive by the adoption and implementation of his reforms. All these factors combine to create an almost insurmountable odds against any opposition group being the catalyst for change in Russia. His reforms. Overcoming resistance is addressed with two points. Visualization and planning are discussed next. The document concludes with a final section summarizing the findings and the roadmap for achieving Navalny's vision. The document concludes with a final section summarizing the findings and the roadmap for achieving Navalny's vision. Creat_LL_GAPTEXT_OP.

9.3. Point 3

To begin with, reforms seek to create a robust system that's resilient to corruption and ensures transparency. In any modernizing state, if you have a strong rule of law and a genuinely fair and decentralized administration, every individual will have an opportunity to affect the direction of their locality and the overall country. The supposed purpose of the Russian state is to create conditions in which all members of our society can have a comfortable and fulfilling life. When you clearly define the role of the central and regional organs of the state, it will be clear to citizens where they can go to access services, finance or to register a business or protest. And yet, acting upon this vision in a meaningful way is currently almost impossible, because the resources for genuine and deep and lasting local self-governance are held back by the culture of top-down corruption that has infected the myriad limbs of the Russian Public Administration. This is not always understood in the EU and other partners of Russia such as the British Government. They may call for Russia to play a more constructive role on the world stage - such as in the conflict in Syria or in international talks on cybersecurity - and they may castigate the Russian retirement of any prolongation of anti-Western sentiment and talk of the special or unique character of the Russian way. But they do not appreciate that there is no 'Russian political tradition', 'Russian values' or 'national idea' in any genuine pluralistic sense, because the festering sore of public administration, the root of true popular involvement, is artificially kept from allowing the values of Russian society to flourish. The artificial corruption of central Russian life has left the ordinary and extraordinary minds of the Russian people voiceless, and has actually driven the country away from any sort of geopolitical partnership. The attempt by the authorities to stymie civil activism on one hand and yet allow ordinary citizens some form of participation on the other; the existence of a set of standards that must be achieved when.

10. CONCLUSION

First, Alexei Navalny has shown us Russia's key problems and has started to develop systematic strategies. Based on his vision, I propose a roadmap to transform his ideas for change into a set of concrete and practical actions, so as to, one day, we can see Russia become a modern, strong and civilized country. This journey might be long and full of barriers and obstacles. The modernization of Russia is by no means an easy task and requires continuous effort and commitment from the society as a whole.

But as given in our section of "Mobilizing supports", Russia, as a nation, has already started to progress. We should keep the momentum and work together in order to make Navalny's vision a reality. In fact, the journey has just begun. There is still a long way for us to go and numerous obstacles to be overcome. But the future of Russia belongs to us. It is time for changes. Thank you for your attention and I hope that you enjoy reading the document as well as have a better understanding of Navalny's vision for a modern Russia.

LEGACY PICTURES OF ALEXIE NAVALNY AND MEMORABLE PICTURES OF YULIA NAVALNAYA

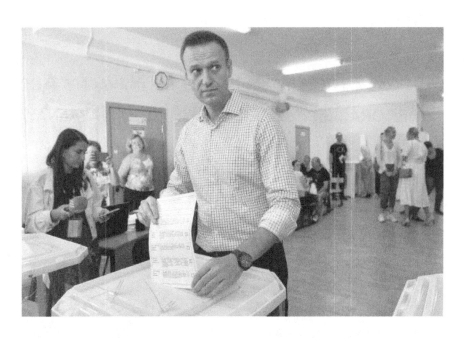

About the Author

Dr. Kofi Frimpong-Aninakwa was the Accountant for over twenty years at the Ghana Export Promotion Authority (GEPA) in Ghana. He worked in collaboration with the treasuries, the Ministries of Trade and Finance, for the preparation of annual budgets on behalf of his organization from 1981.

He undertook his Higher National Diploma (HND) in Accountancy at the Accra Technical University in 1996. When he transitioned to the United States, he had the opportunity of completing his graduate program at the Cambridge College at the satellite campus in Springfield, Massachusetts, in Master's in Business Management in 2014. He undertook his DBA program in Business Management and Entrepreneurship and completed in 2017. He works at the Hartford Public Schools as a Secretary and also as a Private Management Consultant.

He and his family worship as members of the Catholic Ministry at the St. Isaac Joques Ghanaian Catholic Church in East Hartford, Connecticut. His daughter is Dr. Sandra Frimpong-Aninakwa. He has 6 textbooks for secondary business education when he was teaching in Ghana from 1979 in accounting, commercial law, and commerce. He belongs to Kwahuman Association of Connecticut, which has affiliations from his home country Ghana.

Made in the USA
Las Vegas, NV
22 October 2024

10281625R00105